BRUCE WEBER'S INSIDE BASEBALL 1986

SCHOLASTIC INC.
New York Toronto London Auckland Sydney

PHOTO CREDITS

Cover: (left) Photo of Dwight Gooden by Mickey Palmer/Focus on Sports; (right) Photo of John Tudor by Rich Pilling/Focus on Sports. **iv, 6, 11, 15, 30:** New York Yankees. **4, 8, 14, 48, 84:** Kansas City Royals. **7:** Toronto Blue Jays. **9, 34:** Baltimore Orioles. **10, 46:** Chicago White Sox. **12, 52:** Seattle Mariners. **13, 36:** Detroit Tigers. **16, 22, 58, 72:** Los Angeles Dodgers. **18, 25, 26, 60:** New York Mets. **19, 21, 23, 27, 64:** St. Louis Cardinals. **20, 62:** Montreal Expos. **24, 80:** Atlanta Braves. **28:** Jerry Wachter Photography, Ltd. **32:** Action Photographics Inc. **38:** (left) Boston Red Sox; (right) UPI. **40:** Cleveland Indians. **42:** Milwaukee Brewers. **44:** California Angels. **50:** Minnesota Twins. **54:** Oakland A's. **56:** Texas Rangers, jaybo/Miami. **66:** Philadelphia Phillies. **68:** Chicago Cubs. **70:** Pittsburgh Pirates. **74:** San Diego Padres. **76:** Cincinnati Reds. **78:** Houston Astros. **82:** San Francisco Giants.

No part of this publication may be reproduced in whole or in part, or stored in a retrieval system, or transmitted in any form or by any means, electronic, mechanical, photocopying, recording, or otherwise, without written permission of the publisher. For information regarding permission, write to Scholastic Inc., 730 Broadway, New York, NY 10003.

ISBN 0-590-40271-4

Copyright © 1986 by Scholastic Books, Inc. All rights reserved. Published by Scholastic Inc.

12 11 10 9 8 7 6 5 4 3 2 1   3   6 7 8 9/8 0 1/9

Printed in the U.S.A.   01

CONTENTS

Introduction: "Don't Take the A Train" **1**

American League All-Pro Team **5**

National League All-Pro Team **17**

American League Team Previews **29**

National League Team Previews **59**

Statistics 1985 **85**

   American League Batting **86**

   American League Pitching **93**

   National League Batting **96**

   National League Pitching **103**

Bruce Weber Picks How They'll Finish in 1986 **107**

You Pick How They'll Finish in 1986 **108**

With Rickey Henderson getting on base in front of him, the Yanks' Don Mattingly should lead the RBI race again in '86!

INTRODUCTION:
"Don't Take the A Train"

There's an old New York subway joke that goes something like this:

Visitor: How do you get to Carnegie Hall?
Native: Practice. Practice.

The same native wag could probably give similar directions to the 1986 World Series, but only if the questioner is determined to play in the Series.

For the rest of us, directions to the Series should be a bit simpler. From Shea Stadium, take the No. 7 Flushing IRT train to Grand Central Station, then transfer for an uptown No. 4 IRT to Woodlawn/Jerome and get off at 161st Street. That's the stop for Yankee Stadium.

That's the way we see it in 1986, dear reader. It promises to be New York's first Subway Series since 1956, when the Brooklyn Dodgers were beaten by Don Larsen's perfect game and the rest of the Yankees in a seven-game thriller. A couple of seasons later, the Dodgers were off to Los Angeles and, in 1962, when the Mets were born, it became instantly evident that it would be a long time before the next Subway Series.

For a while, it looked like a New York-New York confrontation was a real possibility for 1985. It looked just as likely that a Southern California Freeway Series (Dodgers-Angels) was also in the cards. In the end,

1

however, the cards read Cards vs. Royals in the Interstate 70 Series, won by the western Missouri reps from Kaycee.

That's not the way we see it for '86. We simply do not believe that enough Cardinals can duplicate their '85 performances for St. Louis to make it two in a row. Whitey's guys enjoyed super years all in the same season in winning the NL East crown a year ago. Similarly, the Royals were probably lucky to win the AL West in '85 (though we told you a year ago that they'd win). There's plenty of speed, some great pitching, and some heady managing in Kansas City. But there just isn't enough power in the lineup.

The Dodgers have both power and pitching, but their defense is suspect, which cost them in the League Championship Series. The Angels, an experienced team, might have trouble keeping up the pace in middle to late October. The defending AL East champs in Toronto possibly have the best chance of repeating their division title. But there's a new manager on hand and some real questions about the bullpen.

So we'll go with our Subway Series, matching two bitter rivals who battle all year long, usually in the newspapers. (The best way to get George Steinbrenner to do something in the Bronx is for the Mets to do something in Queens. Boss George hates seeing anyone in the New York headlines except his Yankees.)

It figures to be a great series, matching

baseball's two top first sackers, Don Mattingly and Keith Hernandez; two of the top pitchers, lightning-quick Dr. K, Dwight Gooden, and crafty lefty, Ron Guidry; and established outfield stars like Rickey Henderson and Dave Winfield against tomorrow's star, Darryl Strawberry.

Some final tips on enjoying World Series '86: Buy plenty of subway tokens (the Series could go seven), arrive at the parks early, and be prepared for heavy crowds on the trains. It's still easier than the long ride across Missouri or the LA freeways during rush hour.

And, by the way, if you're still interested, the regular season and League Championship Series should be great, too. Enjoy!

— Bruce Weber

December 16, 1985

Kansas City pitcher Bret Saberhagen would love to duplicate his October '85 performance: a child and a World Series title.

American League
ALL-PRO TEAM

First Base
DON MATTINGLY
NEW YORK YANKEES

New York is, without question, the first-base capital of the United States. In Queens, there's the National League's best, Keith Hernandez of the Mets. In the Bronx, there's the world's best, Don Mattingly of the Yanks, the 1985 American League MVP.

After only 2½ seasons, Mattingly has taken steps toward becoming a Yankee immortal. That's pretty fast company for the 25-year-old. But his incredible bat and artistic glove have qualified him for future induction into the Yankee Hall of Fame.

Look at the numbers. A .324 average (routine for Don), 35 homers (fourth in the league), and 145 RBIs (exceptional in any league). The ribbie mark was the AL's best since Ted Williams and Junior Stephens each had 159 for the 1949 Red Sox.

At the plate, Don has an almost unique ability to drive the ball (not just make contact), wherever it's pitched. That makes him an RBI threat any time there's a runner on base. (That happens frequently when Rickey Henderson is in the lineup.)

Manager Lou Piniella must smile when he considers his major-league managerial debut, knowing that Mattingly is going to help the Yanks win enough games to help him keep his job — until June, at least.

Second Base
DAMASO GARCIA
TORONTO BLUE JAYS

George Steinbrenner can't be thrilled when he watches Toronto in the AL playoffs. Everyone knows that the Yankee boss has been paying Doyle Alexander while the Jays benefited from his 17 wins. But George remembers having Damaso Garcia on his side, too.

A native of the Dominican Republic, Garcia has bloomed in Canada. It took a while, but the Jays were patient. Since coming over from the Yanks in '79, Damaso has become an AL stick-out. He's consistent at bat and in the field, year in and year out. His best season may have been 1982, when he hit .310, with 185 hits, 32 two-baggers, and 54 steals. But he also hit .307 in '83, .284 in '84, and .282 in '85. Now combined with young Tony Fernandez at shortstop, Damaso has given the Jays strength in the middle for years to come.

New manager Jimy Williams knows well what the 28-year-old Garcia can do for him. The 6–0, 175-pound second sacker is an excellent contact man at the plate, the better to hit-and-run with; and he's tremendously steady in the field, which helps the young Jays. Toronto may not repeat in '86, but their solid strength up the middle certainly gives the Jays a real shot.

Third Base
GEORGE BRETT
KANSAS CITY ROYALS

One of these days, an American League manager is going to walk George Brett intentionally with the bases loaded. And he'll tell the press after the game, "Heck, I'd rather give Kansas City one run than three or four."

That's the power of George Brett, possibly the most dangerous hitter in baseball today. He's especially dangerous when Willie Wilson is on base ahead of him and when Hal McRae is wielding a hot bat behind him. But day in and day out, pitchers fear No. 5 in the white-and-blue, striding to the plate.

Opposing managers warn their hurlers "not to let Brett beat you." Which means that George doesn't see many decent pitches. Despite a career high in walks (103), George prefers to swing the bat whenever he can. "I don't like to walk," he says. "Whenever I see a pitch I like, I'll go after it."

Brett's prowess with the stick is nearly matched by his ability in the field. Once a liability with the glove, he's become an outstanding defensive third baseman.

The team leader in batting, slugging, on-base percentage, RBIs, hits, doubles, and walks (along with 30 homers), George is in a class by himself.

Shortstop
CAL RIPKEN
BALTIMORE ORIOLES

In an uncertain period among AL shortstops, 6–4 Cal Ripken, Jr., of the Baltimore Orioles stands tall at the top.

Though the Baltimore-area native did not perform as well at the plate as in the previous two seasons, he remains the Os' most solid citizen. Not that a .282 average, with 26 homers and 110 RBIs, is anything to feel a bit sorry about. In a year when the Birds were mired in fourth place, 16 games off the pace, Ripken was the key to a potentially powerful lineup. Next year?

The son of long-time Oriole coach Cal Ripken, Sr., grew up around the Orioles and Baltimore. He still donates game tickets to underprivileged kids and senior citizens every time they open the gates at Memorial Stadium.

Playing a position where power is practically unknown, the 200-pounder is capable of driving the ball every time he comes to bat.

There are some outstanding young shortstops in the AL, including Toronto's Tony Fernandez, a consistent hitter who is developing consistency in the field. But he'll have to catch Cal Ripken who, at age 25 and with four seasons behind him, is the key to an Oriole revival in 1986.

Outfield
HAROLD BAINES
CHICAGO WHITE SOX

Credit the White Sox's scouting department. They picked Harold Baines at the top of the June 1977 draft, and he has been doing All-Star work ever since.

In a league chock full of great outfielders, Baines remains among our All-Pro choices, as much for his durability as for his ability. Harold made it into the White Sox lineup for 160 games last season; he simply never takes a day off. Oh, he'll miss a couple of games here and there, but when manager Tony LaRussa needs him, he's ready to play.

In Baines's sixth major-league season a year ago, the 6–2, 175-pounder had his best year with the stick, hitting .309 with 198 hits, both career highs and both among the league's top half dozen. He also swatted 22 homers and banged 29 doubles and knocked in 113 runs, trailing only Don Mattingly, Eddie Murray, and Dave Winfield, power hitters of note.

Interestingly, Baines is now entering his eighth full season in pro ball and his eighth year managed by Sox boss Tony LaRussa. An excellent fielder and a now-respected power man, Baines's continued success is the key to the Chicago hopes of making the 1986 pennant battle.

Outfield
RICKEY HENDERSON
NEW YORK YANKEES

Looking for one player who can make things happen? Try Yankee center fielder Rickey Henderson.

The Bronx swiftie, who came to New York in a seven-player deal with the A's before the '85 season, was often the sparkplug that ignited the Yankee machine. Though his batting average tailed off from the .350's in July to .314 at season's end, he still brought excitement to Yankee Stadium every time he reached base.

You can bet that Don Mattingly was overjoyed to see the 27-year-old Henderson ahead of him in the Yankee lineup. It's no accident that Rickey led the league in runs scored (146) while Mattingly was tops in RBIs with 145. Cal Ripken, the AL's No. 2 run-scorer, finished 30 behind Rickey.

Though some question Henderson's concentration, and there are other questions about his poststrike absence last year, there's no arguing with his flashy on-field performance. Though his 80 stolen bases were 50 behind his all-time record of 130, Rickey still set a Yankee club record. "Stolen bases aren't as important here," he said. "I don't have to be on third base in order to score with this club." With his speed, Rickey is a threat to score from anywhere.

Outfield
PHIL BRADLEY
SEATTLE MARINERS

The Mariners' Phil Bradley is 6–0 and weighs 175 pounds. Entirely too small — for the NFL! A record-breaking quarterback at the U. of Missouri, Bradley quickly realized that he couldn't make it in pro football. So he turned to baseball, and Seattle hasn't spent one unhappy moment about Bradley's decision.

The 27-year-old really blossomed in '85, swatting the ball at a .300 clip, good for seventh in the AL. The big improvement, however, came in the power department. The one-time singles hitter turned slugger, with 26 homers and 88 RBIs. Incredibly, despite nearly 400 major-league at-bats, Bradley had never hit a big-league homer before last season.

Bradley credits Seattle Mariner hitting coach — and one-time big-league slugger — Deron Johnson for his power show in '85. Johnson made a couple of adjustments in Bradley's batting stance and mental approach to hitting. The rest, as they say, is pleasant history.

"I'd always hit well," says Bradley. "I was over .300 every year in the minors and right at .300 as a big-league rookie. No one ever mentioned long ball. I'm glad that Deron Johnson did."

Catcher
LANCE PARRISH
DETROIT TIGERS

If this were a 1985 postseason All-Pro Team, the catcher's spot would belong to Carlton Fisk. The White Sox catcher did not hit for average (only .238), but did swat 37 homers and banged in 107 runs, joining All-Pro Harold Baines as Chicago's plate leaders. But off-season reports had Fisk on the move for 1986, with Joel Skinner becoming the Sox catcher. Thus, this vote for Parrish, for the third straight year.

On balance, the National League appears to be blessed with better catching strength than the AL. Still, it's hard to dispute Parrish's credentials.

The coming season will be the tenth in Detroit for Parrish, who will turn 30 at midyear. Though the Tigers slumped to third place, 15 games back, in '85, it was a bounce-back year for Parrish, who went from .237 in '84 to .273 in '85. That was 11 points better than his career mark. He added 28 homers, his third-best power year, and banged in 98 runs for the second year in a row.

The 6–3, 210-pounder is among the best defensively, with one of the most feared arms in the game. And he's durable, too, averaging 147 games per year the last three seasons.

Righthanded Pitcher
BRET SABERHAGEN
KANSAS CITY ROYALS

On a Sunday night in late October in Kansas City, Bret Saberhagen ruled the world. Just before Game 6 of the World Series, as the nation waited, Mrs. Saberhagen made Bret, who doesn't even look 21, a father. Then, in Game 7, Bret spun a tidy five-hit shutout as the Royals climbed all over the Cards to complete their stunning championship comeback.

This is, obviously, the age of the infant pitching ace. While Saberhagen has risen to the top of the AL righties, 21-year-old Dwight Gooden has become the NL's — and the game's — best. The Cy Young Award winners have never been younger.

Saberhagen may not have all of Gooden's tools, but he does possess amazing baseball savvy for one so young. And his arm is amazingly live. Over the last three months of last season, he was virtually unhittable. And his Series performance, 18 innings, 11 hits, one run, made him a household word.

"He reminds me of a young Catfish Hunter," says Royal pitching coach Gary Blaylock of Saberhagen. "He has mastered four pitches, can zip his fastball at around 92 miles per hour, and knows more than he needs to about pitching."

Lefthanded Pitcher
RON GUIDRY
NEW YORK YANKEES

You can't blame Ron Guidry for feeling pretty good about the 1986 season. He didn't feel at all well before the '85 campaign.

There was plenty of self-doubt a year ago, following an awful (for Guidry) 10–11 record and 4.51 ERA in 1984. The Gator, as the Louisiana native is called, had gone from power pitcher to control pitcher, and had sunk to the depths after his 25–3 Cy Young season in 1978. Could Guidry come back?

You bet. "It took me a while to get my act back together," Guidry says. "I used to blow the ball by people with my smoke and my slider. Now I have to work at it."

Guidry credits an improved Yankee defense for his 1985 improvement. But you just can't give better play in the field all of the credit for a 22–6 mark (17-game turnaround), a 3.27 ERA, and a strikeout-to-walk ratio of 143–42 in 259 tough innings.

Now, at age 35, Guidry is crafty as well as good. It's an excellent combination. And at 5–11 and only 162 pounds, Guidry needs all the smarts he can get.

"A lot of people thought I was all through after that 1984 performance. I had to show them," says Guidry. "I think it made me work even harder last year."

The third-base experiment behind him, the Dodgers' Pedro Guerrero should improve on his outstanding 1985 season.

National League ALL-PRO TEAM

First Base
KEITH HERNANDEZ
NEW YORK METS

In New York, home of great artists in the worlds of music, art, and theater, Met first sacker Keith Hernandez takes his place with the very best.

There may never have been a slicker fielder at the position than the 32-year-old veteran. His glove-work is often nothing less than sensational, turning certain base hits into outs — and double plays!

At the plate, the 6–0, 195-pounder is more than at home. Early last season, Keith's father, watching a Met game on TV at home in California, noted that he couldn't see the "7" on Keith's No. 17 uniform when Keith was in his batting stance. At the time, Keith, a former NL batting champ, was struggling around .250. Those aren't the numbers of a hitting leader.

Armed with his father's scouting report, Keith made the necessary adjustment and started tattooing the ball all around the league. He finished at .309, sixth in the NL, raising his average nearly 20 points in the last two crucial weeks of the season. He also had 91 RBIs and an all-time record of 24 game-winning RBIs. Talk about Mr. Clutch!

For the Mets to win in '86, Keith will have to do at least as well again.

Second Base
TOMMY HERR
ST. LOUIS CARDINALS

Tommy Herr is sure to be the American Medical Association's Player of the Year. A 1983 knee operation might have ended Tommy's career. But Tommy wasn't listening, which, as much as anything, explains the Cards' unexpected supremacy in the NL last year.

Now, at age 29, Tommy has stepped to the head of the class at second base in the National League. He's the perfect man in the perfect spot in the Card lineup. There's speed and quickness ahead of him, with All-Pro Willie McGee (and his .353 average) and Vince Coleman (110 stolen bases). Those two set the table for Herr, who responded with a .302 average and 110 RBIs, more than the last three years combined. He also stole 31 bases and finished third in doubles with 38. Not bad for someone who had been written off a couple of years earlier.

Lack of power (only eight homers) is about the only element keeping the 6-0, 185-pounder out of superstar country. He combines with the all-timer at short, Ozzie Smith, to give the Cards great strength up the middle. The All-Pro duo allowed manager Whitey Herzog to sleep more easily this off-season.

Third Base
TIM WALLACH
MONTREAL EXPOS

It used to be easy to pick the NL third sacker. Mike Schmidt. The Phillie slugger owned the spot for years. But he played 1B in '85, so 3B is up for grabs.

You can make a case for a variety of players, but most are too old, too young, or too inconsistent. Tim Wallach of Montreal is none of these, with new emphasis on the consistent.

At age 27, the lanky 6-3, 200-pounder has finally made his mark. His glove has become a major asset. (His fielding percentage has improved every season for the last four years.) "It doesn't surprise me," says Wallach. "Those who've knocked my fielding in the past didn't know what they were talking about."

But Tim's major improvement came at the plate. In '85, he hit .260, 14 points better than the previous year. And he also swatted 22 homers and knocked in 81 runs, also major improvements.

It's doubtful that Wallach could have beaten out Graig Nettles or Ron Cey in their prime. And youngsters like Terry Pendleton are ready to assume Schmidt's old title. But, as long as Wallach remains consistent and improves on past performance, he could well be the NL's main guy at third.

Shortstop
OZZIE SMITH
ST. LOUIS CARDINALS

Managers often warn pitchers, "Don't let this guy beat you." Depending on where you are, "this guy" can be Jack Clark or George Brett or Gary Carter or Dave Parker. It never is Ozzie Smith.

But after the Wizard of Oz's game-winning homer in the fifth game of the NL playoffs, the 30-year-old earned a new degree of respect. Solid-citizen Smith is an unquestioned leader on the field for St. Louis. No one, probably no one ever, has played shortstop like this acrobat. His brilliant leaps must drive ballet dancers crazy. And his glove-work is simply artistic. Brimming with quiet confidence, he's the glue that holds the Cards together.

When Card owner Gussie Busch inked a two-million-dollar-a-year contract with Ozzie before the '86 season, baseball experts buzzed. Who signs a Punch-and-Judy hitter to a two-million-buck contract? "Gussie's finally gone off the deep end," they said.

Forget it. Ozzie put together his finest season ever, hitting .276, far above his .243 lifetime average. He also banged six homers (plus the play-off winner), stole 31 bases, and got the Cards to within a couple of outs of a world title.

Outfield
PEDRO GUERRERO
LOS ANGELES DODGERS

Remember how Kaycee Royal opponents lived in fear of George Brett during the 1985 postseason? That's exactly how Dodger rivals treat Pedro Guerrero.

Now that the Guerrero third-base experiment seems finally over, there's no reason to believe that anyone will take his place in the NL All-Pro outfield for years to come.

Manager Tommy Lasorda only wishes that he could recapture Guerrero's June 1985 performance and bottle it. The Dodgers were 5½ games off the pace when Lasorda returned Pedro to the Dodger outfield. In June, his 15 homers and 27 RBIs enabled him to raise his batting mark from .268 to .324. Only Babe Ruth, Roger Maris, and Indian Bob Johnson (who?) had ever hit 15 dingers in June before. Pedro sizzled again in July with a .460 bat mark, as LA zoomed to the top of the NL West.

In a league blessed with great outfielders — Willie McGee, Dave Parker, Tim Raines, Dale Murphy, and more — Guerrero, the Dodger smoothie, is the main man. His .320 average and 33 round-trippers, despite nagging injuries and the upsetting stay at third base, make him a great man to pitch around whenever the Dodgers come to town.

Outfield
WILLIE McGEE
ST. LOUIS CARDINALS

Imagine a Yankee outfield with Dave Winfield, Willie McGee, and Rickey Henderson. Could have been — except for a 1981 trade that sent Willie, the 1985 National League MVP, from the Yankees to the Cards for pitcher Bob Sykes. (Who?)

Willie made it to the Cards' big club the next season, played a major role in the '82 play-offs and World Series, then was the major cog in the 1985 NL championship machine.

McGee, at age 27, has arrived. His .353 mark in '85 not only led the NL, but was the best ever by a National League switch-hitter. Combined with speedy Vince Coleman, the Cards had the best one-two base-stealing punch in the majors. Together they stole 166 bases, 56 by Willie. Defensively, they were murder, too. McGee, in center, ran down everything. "If he can't catch it," says manager Whitey Herzog, "it simply cannot be caught." In tandem with left fielder Coleman, the left side of the Card outfield was no-man's land for opposing hitters.

Though Willie labored long (six years) in the Yankee farm chain, he wasn't exactly unknown. His last year, at Nashville (Southern League), he hit a team-leading .322. The team's No. 2 hitter? Don Mattingly.

Outfield
DALE MURPHY
ATLANTA BRAVES

Dale Murphy, winner of the NL MVP Award in 1982 and 1983, had to like the changes owner Ted Turner made at the top of the Braves' organization. With Bobby Cox now at the head of the front office and Chuck Tanner in the field office, the Braves have taken steps to return to respectability. Their highly respectable center fielder has to be pleased.

Though Dale tailed off somewhat last season after a blazing start, he still scared enemy pitchers every time. The 6–5, 215-pounder wound up hitting .300, 10th in the league. He also smacked 37 homers — after three straight years of 36 — to lead the NL. He was the leading run-scorer (118), fifth in hits (185), fifth in on-base percentage (.388), third in slugging (.539), and second in RBIs (111). All-Pro numbers to be sure, especially for a gifted fielder who was a catcher through the 1979 season.

Trouble is, the National League is loaded with outfielders, including seven of the league's top 10 hitters in '85. And, except for game-winning RBIs (Keith Hernandez led the league), every offensive category in the NL was led by an outfielder. So, with apologies to fans of Dave Parker and Timmy Raines, we'll stick with the biggest Brave.

Catcher
GARY CARTER
NEW YORK METS

If Gary Carter can play without pain this season, there's no telling how much he can do for the New York Mets.

Gary played in terrible pain over the final three months of the '85 season, after a pre-All-Star knee injury threatened to end his season early. But the Mets were in the thick of the NL East race, and Carter said, "Let's wait until after the season for surgery."

Though the pain was obvious on the strapping 6–2, 210-pounder's face, both at-bat and behind the plate, he hung in there, playing in 149 games, most of them as the full-time catcher. His leadership pulled Dwight Gooden and the rest of the mound staff through the season. And his personal performance took the Mets to the next-to-last day of the season before they bowed out of the pennant race.

Though Gary ended up with a more-than-satisfactory .281 average, a team-leading 32 homers, and an even 100 RBIs, few Met fans will forget his West Coast homer binge. The 31-year-old banged five homers in two games, and eight in six outings. It provided a timely lift for the club.

New York can't wait to see a healthy Gary Carter.

Righthanded Pitcher
DWIGHT GOODEN
NEW YORK METS

Is there a baseball fan in America who wouldn't swap for Dwight Gooden's future? Or his past?

At age 21, the 1985 Cy Young winner is already the No. 1 pitcher in the game. He owns a fistful of records. He has the blazing fastball and the enormous curve. He has incredible control. He has even learned how to hold opposing base runners (there usually aren't many) close to their bases. The youngster from Tampa, Florida, can do it all.

The only way Dwight can fail is through not meeting fans' expectations. Met fans (and Gooden fans) expect the 6–2, 210-pounder to strike out 10 or more every game. (He did average 8.73 strikeouts per nine innings.) They expect him to shut out the opponents every game. (He did have eight shutouts, second only to St. Louis's John Tudor.) They expect him to toss a no-hitter. (We believe that he will, soon.) They expect him to win every five days. (He did go 24–4.)

This is a brilliant young man and a brilliant athlete. If he stays healthy, he will own the record books someday, and he will lead the Mets to pennants and the World Series. The man who already owns both velocity and location is awesome!

Lefthanded Pitcher
JOHN TUDOR
ST. LOUIS CARDINALS

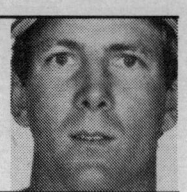

Forget the final game of the World Series. (John and Whitey have.) Without John Tudor, the Cardinals would have been watching the Series on TV.

The much-traveled lefty, who's in St. Louis to stay, pulled one of the most remarkable comebacks in baseball history last season. And with his newly demonstrated skills, he's likely to remain one of the top NL hurlers.

After coming to the Cards from Pittsburgh last season, Tudor proceeded to lose seven of his first eight starts. Wow, 1–7! Another stiff.

Then came the miraculous turnaround. Tudor, who possesses those two key skills — velocity (speed) and location (hits the corners), won 20 of his last 21. His 21–8 mark put him just behind the Mets' superkid, Dwight Gooden. He had 14 complete games, a league-leading 10 shutouts, and 169 strikeouts. Not bad for someone whose fastball only clocks 87 miles per hour. But Tudor has great stuff, nibbles away at the plate, and walked only 49 in 275 innings. His 10-inning, 1–0 win over the Mets in September (no New Yorker reached second base) helped nail down the NL East. The 6–0, 185-pounder dominates ball games.

Though the Orioles' pitching must improve for the Birds to get into the '86 race, veteran 1B Eddie Murray will star again.

American League TEAM PREVIEWS

AL East
NEW YORK YANKEES
1985 Finish: Second
1986 Prediction: First

Willie Randolph

Brian Fisher

Both Billy Martin and Yogi Berra have vowed never to manage the Yankees again, giving hope to new manager Lou Piniella.

Lou could, of course, lower the heat considerably by winning early and often. The talent is there. AL MVP Don Mattingly (.324, 145 RBIs) is the world's No. 1 first sacker, and Willie Randolph (.276) seems to be fairly set at second. It's unlikely that Bobby Meacham (.218) will return to shortstop without a fight, but Jim Pagliarulo (.239) is ready to be the everyday third sacker. Versatile ex-Indian Mike Fischlin can spell them all.

Yankee fans hope that Boss Steinbrenner can make peace with RF Dave Winfield (.275, 114 RBIs), still a key to the Yankee fortunes. He joins Mattingly and lightning-quick CF Rickey Henderson (.314, 80 steals) to give the Yanks the best 1–2–3 punch in the game. Power-hitting Dan Pasqua or ex-Oriole Gary Roenicke get a shot in LF.

Pending later developments, there were problems in the catching department. Butch Wynegar (.223), a free agent, may re-sign, but backup Ron Hassey (.296) was dealt to the White Sox.

Despite the Yanks' team ERA of 3.69, third best in the AL, pitching remains the major question mark. We believe that lefty Ron Guidry (22–6) can do it again, and ex-White Sox Britt Burns should be a major plus. But Joe Cowley is off to Chicago, and the rest of the crowd is unsteady. Dave Righetti (12–7, 29 saves) could return from the bullpen, if Rod Scurry is ready to help Brian Fisher, who had a great year. And which, if any, Niekro will be back?

With some righthanded power, a starting pitcher, some catching help, and a shortstop, Lou could enjoy a lovely summer.

STAT LEADERS — 1985

BATTING
Average: Mattingly, .324
Runs: Henderson, 146*
Hits: Mattingly, 211
Doubles: Mattingly, 48*
Triples: Winfield, 6
Home Runs: Mattingly, 35
RBIs: Mattingly, 145*
Game-Winning RBIs: Mattingly, 21*
Stolen Bases: Henderson, 80*

PITCHING
Wins: Guidry, 22*
Losses: P. Niekro, 12
Complete Games: Guidry, 11
Shutouts: Guidry, Whitson, 2
Saves: Righetti, 29
Walks: P. Niekro, 120
Strikeouts: P. Niekro, 149

*Led league.

AL East
TORONTO BLUE JAYS
1985 Finish: First
1986 Prediction: Second

Tony Fernandez   **Jesse Barfield**

Despite the disappointment of the final games of the AL Championship Series, 1985 was a very good year in eastern Canada. We are not predicting another postseason celebration in '86. But, if it happened, no one would be shocked.

The first Blue Jay shocker has already occurred. AL Manager of the Year Bobby Cox, who lifted the Jays out of the depths of the AL East, is no longer a manager, toiling instead in the Atlanta Braves' front office. But Toronto believes that young Jimy Williams is ready to fill his shoes.

Why not? There's plenty of talent around Exhibition Stadium, and just a few real problems. Williams will probably make some changes in the bullpen, where Bill Caudill (4–6, 14 saves) never became a dominating force. Luis Leal (3–6, 5.75) and Gary Lavelle (5–7) are both in trouble. And there's the designated hitter spot. The '85 Jays tried lots of folks, without real success. If the new DH has a touch of speed, too, it will be that much better. In addition, a lefty starter and possibly a catcher would help.

Otherwise, total joy. Four-year starter Willie Upshaw should return at first, though his name was mentioned in trade rumors. The middle is in great shape with All-Pro 2B Damaso Garcia (.282) and young SS Tony Fernandez (.289). The 3B platoon of Garth Iorg (.313) and Rance Mulliniks (.295) is outstanding. The Jays, never very powerful in the past, discovered new power in OFs George Bell (.275, 28 homers), Jesse Barfield (.289, 27 homers), and Lloyd Moseby (.259, 18 homers). Starting pitching is in decent shape, with righty Dave Stieb (14–13, 2.48), lefty Jimmy Key (14–6), and Doyle Alexander (17–10). Jim Clancy (9–6) is a question mark.

STAT LEADERS — 1985

BATTING
Average: Barfield, .289
Runs: Barfield, 94
Hits: Garcia, 169
Doubles: Barfield, 34
Triples: Fernandez, 10
Home Runs: Bell, 28
RBIs: Bell, 95
Game-Winning RBIs: Barfield, 12
Stolen Bases: Moseby, 37

PITCHING
Wins: Alexander, 17
Losses: Stieb, 13
Complete Games: Stieb, 8
Shutouts: Stieb, 2
Saves: Caudill, 14
Walks: Stieb, 96
Strikeouts: Stieb, 167

AL East
BALTIMORE ORIOLES
1985 Finish: Fourth
1986 Prediction: Third

Eddie Murray   **Don Aase**

For Earl Weaver to succeed in his second go-round as Oriole manager, he'll have to see a lot less of the team doctor and the New York Yankees. The O's and Yanks played 13 times during Earl's half season, and Baltimore won — once! Meanwhile, the doc tended to the needs of such leading Birds as Mike Boddicker, Storm Davis, Fred Lynn, Lee Lacy, and John Shelby, among others.

Assuming healthy players in Maryland, the 1986 O's should present a potent lineup, needing only consistent pitching to challenge for the crown. 1B Eddie Murray, owner of a new five-year, $13-million contract, hit .297 a year ago, with 31 homers and a career-high 124 RBIs. He's super. Earl should be able to control 2B Alan Wiggins, the onetime troubled Padre who hit .285 with 30 steals in 76 Oriole outings. SS Cal Ripken (.282, 15 game-winning RBIs) is the AL's best, with Floyd Rayford (.306 in 105 games) the probable solution at third.

Sound seasons from Lacy (.293 in 121 games) and Lynn (.263, 68 RBIs in 124 games) should do wonders for shoring up the outfield. The O's hit a league-high 214 homers a year ago. But their pitching did them in.

Look for Mike Boddicker (12–17), once the AL's top righty; Storm Davis (10–8); Scotty McGregor (14–14, 4.81 ERA); and Mike Flanagan (4–5, 5.13 ERA), once the league's top lefty, to turn things around in '86. Flanagan missed half the season last year, and Boddicker's knee tendinitis cost him his last four starts. Don Aase (10–6, 14 saves), the bullpen leader, gets help from ex-Yank Rich Bordi. C Rick Dempsey (.254) needs some help. Look for Bill Swaggerty to get a shot at a starting pitcher's spot, and Kelly Paris and newcomer Rex Hudler, in the O's infield.

STAT LEADERS — 1985

BATTING
Average: Murray, .297
Runs: Ripken, 116
Hits: Ripken, 181
Doubles: Murray, 37
Triples: Ripken, 5
Home Runs: Murray, 31
RBIs: Murray, 124
Game-Winning RBIs: Murray, Ripken, 15
Stolen Bases: Wiggins, 30

PITCHING
Wins: McGregor, 14
Losses: Boddicker, 17
Complete Games: Boddicker, 9
Shutouts: Boddicker, 2
Saves: Aase, 14
Walks: Boddicker, 89
Strikeouts: Boddicker, 135

AL East
DETROIT TIGERS
1985 Finish: Third
1986 Prediction: Fourth

Jack Morris   **Lou Whitaker**

Manager Sparky Anderson did a super job at the 1985 World Series. Unfortunately, he did it in the radio broadcast booth. He would have much preferred a much lower perch, like in the dugout.

Sparky's mighty Tigers, winners of 35 of their first 40 games in 1984 on their way to a world title, came back to the pack in '85. They did it with poor defense, spotty relief pitching, and so-so hitting from two or three positions. With a few adjustments and a key player or two, the problems can be solved.

Starting pitching seems to be in good shape. Detroit had a 3.78 team ERA, fourth in the AL in '85. Jack Morris (16–11, 13 complete games) remains one of the league's classiest. Dan Petry (15–13), ex-Met Walt Terrell (15–10), and much-traveled Frank

Tanana (12–14) are set, along with lefty Dave LaPoint. Detroit gave the Giants C Bob Melvin and P Juan Berenguer for LaPoint, only 7–17 for the pitiful Giants, who scored only 29 runs in Dave's 17 losses.

Though the Tigers have problems at 3B, the rest of the infield is super. True, 1B Darrell Evans will be 39 in May, but, at age 38, he slugged 40 homers, becoming the AL's oldest homer king. Lou Whitaker (.279) and Alan Trammell (.258) are excellent at second and short.

The outfield, on the other hand, could be in trouble. Speedy Dave Collins, acquired from the A's, is expected to play left, despite his defensive shortcomings. Chet Lemon's season (.265) made neither Lemon nor Anderson happy. The most consistent outfielder was RF Kirk Gibson (.287, 97 RBIs, 29 homers, 30 steals). But he was on the free-agent market. C Lance Parrish (.273, 98 RBIs) is outstanding.

STAT LEADERS — 1985

BATTING
Average: Gibson, .287
Runs: Whitaker, 102
Hits: Whitaker, 170
Doubles: Gibson, 37
Triples: Whitaker, 8
Home Runs: Evans, 40*
RBIs: Parrish, 98
Game-Winning RBIs: Parrish, 16
Stolen Bases: Gibson, 30

PITCHING
Wins: Morris, 16
Losses: Petry, 13
Complete Games: Morris, 13
Shutouts: Morris, 4
Saves: Hernandez, 31
Walks: Morris, 110
Strikeouts: Morris, 191

*Led league.

AL East
BOSTON RED SOX
1985 Finish: Fifth
1986 Prediction: Fifth

Tony Armas   **Jim Rice**

Boston manager John McNamara should be under pressure to produce this time 'round in Beantown, but he probably doesn't have the horses to do it.

Certainly, he can count on another super season from Wade Boggs, perhaps the best pure hitter in the world today. 3B Boggs, whose glove-work has also improved, smacked the ball at a .368 pace in '85, to win his second AL bat crown. He has never hit less than .325 in the majors. But his mate on the left side of the infield, SS Jackie Gutierrez (.218), was traded to Baltimore for relief pitcher Sammy Stewart. 1B Bill Buckner (.299) went over the 200-hit mark for the second time in his career (201). Marty Barrett (.266) may not be the long-range answer at second base.

There could be changes via trades in the outfield, where Jim Rice (.291, despite missing the last 15 games with a left knee injury), Tony Armas (.265, only 23 homers, in a disappointing year), and Dwight Evans (.263) still make a potent trio. Note that the Sox hit .282 as a team and were still victimized, especially by a porous defense. C Rich Gedman (.295) continues to surprise those who thought he'd never make it big. He threw out nearly half of the runners who tried to steal on him.

A healthy Roger Clemens (7–5, 3.29) will help the pitching staff. Oil Can Boyd (15–13) might have won 20, except for a streak of six winless weeks. Ex-Met farm reliever Wes Gardner could be the closer the Sox need in the bullpen. Ex-Oriole Sammy Stewart (3.61, 9 saves) should also help. Another ex-Met, Calvin Schiraldi, could start, as may Jeff Sellers (14–7 at New Britain) or Rob Woodward. Look for Rey Quinonez to get a shot at short.

STAT LEADERS — 1985

BATTING
Average: Boggs, .368*
Runs: Evans, 110
Hits: Boggs, 240*
Doubles: Buckner, 46
Triples: Gedman, 5
Home Runs: Evans, 29
RBIs: Buckner, 110
Game-Winning RBIs: Evans, 13
Stolen Bases: Buckner, 18

PITCHING
Wins: Boyd, 15
Losses: Hurst, Boyd, 13
Complete Games: Boyd, 13
Shutouts: Boyd, 3
Saves: Crawford, 12
Walks: Lollar, 98
Strikeouts: Hurst, 189

*Led league.

AL East
CLEVELAND INDIANS
1985 Finish: Seventh
1986 Prediction: Sixth

Brett Butler

Julio Franco

Pat Corrales must be feeling pretty good. Despite a club-record 102 losses and a last-place finish in '85, Corrales is set as the Tribe manager for '86 and, it seems, for future years as well.

Actually, the Cleveland tepee is in decent shape. If '85's wounded, like 1B Pat Tabler, OF Mel Hall, and P Ernie Camacho, get healthy, some of those 80,000 seats at Municipal Stadium could actually be filled.

The infield is nearly set. A healthy Tabler (.275 in 117 games) may be able to hold off slugging rookie Jim Wilson at 1B. Free-agent Tony Bernazard (.274) should re-sign and return at 2B. SS Julio Franco (.288, 90 RBIs) is among the AL's better shortstops, and Brook Jacoby (.274, 20 homers, 87 RBIs) is among the AL's better third sackers.

Though there are still some questions about Mel Hall's injured neck, the rest of the outfield is in good hands with Joe Carter (.262, 15 homers) and surprisingly good Brett Butler (.311, 106 runs). This group could be among the league's best.

The major problems arise in that 60'6" corridor between the mound and the plate. Catching is in marginal condition, particularly in terms of offensive production. And the pitching staff's team ERA of 4.92 was the worst in captivity.

Manager Corrales hopes that Roy Smith, whose 2.39 ERA was the best in the International League, can do the same against big-league hitting. Righty Keith Creel (2–5) showed improvement at the end of '85, and Don Schulze (4–10) also began to perk up late. Neil Heaton, the team's lefty ace (9–17) should return.

STAT LEADERS — 1985

BATTING
Average: Butler, .311
Runs: Butler, 106
Hits: Butler, 184
Doubles: Franco, 33
Triples: Butler, 14
Home Runs: Thornton, 22
RBIs: Franco, 90
Game-Winning RBI's: Franco, 9
Stolen Bases: Butler, 47

PITCHING*
Wins: Heaton, 9
Losses: Heaton, 17
Complete Games: Heaton, 5
Shutouts: Heaton, 1
Saves: Waddell, 9
Walks: Heaton, 80
Strikeouts: Wardle, 84

*Bert Blyleven, who was the Indian (and, in several categories, the AL) leader, completed the season with the Minnesota Twins. His figures are found in the Twins' preview.

AL East
MILWAUKEE BREWERS
1985 Finish: Sixth
1986 Prediction: Seventh

Robin Yount

Paul Molitor

George Bamberger deserves better. In his second stint as Brewer manager, Bambi suffers from poor defense, so-so arms, and quiet bats. The only saving grace is that the Milwaukee farm system seems to be on the verge of producing some candidates for the big club's roster.

Defensively, the Brewers allowed more than 100 unearned runs a year ago. Combined with the staff's team earned run average of 4.39, it made consistent winning impossible. The offense's decreased run production only added to their woes.

Of all the Brewers, only Robin Yount, the one-time wonder-kid shortstop who will probably open 1986 in the outfield, and Paul Molitor are certain to be in the Brewer lineup. 1B Cecil Cooper (.293, 99 RBIs) is still among the AL's best. But he could be valuable trade bait. Rookie SS Earnest Riles (.286) was outstanding.

Moving Yount (.277, 68 RBIs, only 122 games) to the outfield will open up some new possibilities, including a deal involving former All-Pro Ben Oglivie (.290, 61 RBIs, 101 games). Billy Joe Robidoux, who led the Texas League with a .342 average, 132 RBIs, 112 runs, and 23 homers, should get a shot at a starting post. (Milwaukee was outhomered in '85, 175–101.) Rookies Carlos Ponce and Doug Loman may also be readying bids for the Brewer outfield. C Ted Simmons (.273) should be back.

Except for Ted Higuera (15–8, 3.90) and Danny Darwin (8–18, 3.80), the pitching is in sorry shape. Darwin lost six games in '85 when the Brewers were shut out. Talk about nonsupport. Youngsters Tim Leary, Tom Candiotti, and Bill Wegman will get a shot at staff positions. Ex-Red Sox Mark Clear could replace released Rollie Fingers.

STAT LEADERS — 1985

BATTING
Average: Molitor, .297
Runs: Molitor, 93
Hits: Cooper, 185
Doubles: Cooper, 39
Triples: Cooper, 8
Home Runs: Cooper, 16
RBIs: Cooper, 99
Game-Winning RBIs: Simmons, 12
Stolen Bases: Molitor, 21

PITCHING
Wins: Higuera, 15
Losses: Darwin, 18
Complete Games: Darwin, 11
Shutouts: Higuera, 2
Saves: Fingers, 17
Walks: Cocanower, 73
Strikeouts: Higuera, 127

AL West
CALIFORNIA ANGELS
1985 Finish: Second
1986 Prediction: First

Mike Witt **Gary Pettis**

Will the 25th time be the charm? Angel manager Gene Mauch has managed 24 previous seasons without ever winning a pennant. No other manager in baseball history can make that sad claim. But the Angels have a decent shot at the AL West title in 1986 and, after that, who knows?

Problem is, the Angels were the AL's worst-hitting team in 1985, and even some outstanding pitching couldn't make up for it. (What is encouraging, however, is that World Champion Kansas City hit only one point better.)

The Angels are okay up the middle with catcher Bob Boone, shortshop Dick Schofield, and center fielder Gary Pettis. The 38-year-old Boone hit .248 and played well defensively. Still, the Angels spent the off-season shopping for catching help. Schofield, a .194 career hitter before the '85 season, hit .219, a major improvement. He's dynamite in the field. And Pettis stole 56 bases while anchoring the outfield defense.

There's plenty of concern about 3B Doug DeCinces's injured back. If the .244 hitter can't go, Jack Howell (.197) may have to fill in again.

It was essential for the Angels to re-sign reliever Donnie Moore (8–8, 31 saves), a free agent. 2B Bobby Grich (.242), a great club leader on and off the field, will be back. But all-time hitter 1B Rod Carew (.280) won't, opening the way for Darryl Sconiers (.286) or farmhand Wally Joyner.

Look for Gus Polidor to get a shot at shortstop and a chance for Urbano Lugo and Curt Kaufman as pitchers. The rest of the mound staff — Mike Witt, Ron Romanick, Don Sutton, Kirk McCaskill, Stew Cliburn, and John Candelaria — seems set.

STAT LEADERS — 1985

BATTING
Average: Beniquez, .304
Runs: Downing, 80
Hits: Downing, 137
Doubles: Jackson, 27
Triples: Pettis, 8
Home Runs: Jackson, 27
RBIs: Downing, Jackson, 85
Game-Winning RBIs: Downing, 12
Stolen Bases: Pettis, 56

PITCHING
Wins: Witt, 15
Losses: McCaskill, 12
Complete Games: Witt, Romanick, McCaskill, 6
Shutouts: Six with 1 each
Saves: Moore, 31
Walks: Witt, 98
Strikeouts: Witt 98

AL West
CHICAGO WHITE SOX
1985 Finish: Third
1986 Prediction: Second

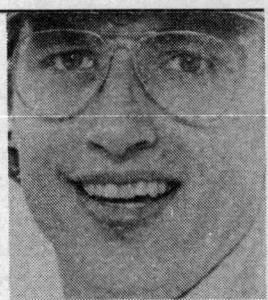

Harold Baines **Ron Kittle**

Ken (Hawk) Harrelson, one of the most colorful and controversial players of his day, now scrambles from the Sox broadcast booth to the front office. The team's new vice-president will handle baseball matters, including personnel — which says it all at this time of year.

It seems that manager Tony LaRussa and Harrelson aren't the best of friends, so the manager's situation should be watched in '86. With Carlton (Pudge) Fisk (.238, but 37 homers) ready to move on, there's a great opportunity for talented youngster Joel Skinner (.341 in 22 games) behind the plate. Ex-Yank Ron Hassey should get plenty of playing time.

The Sox suffered in the DH department until late last season when Ron Kittle got hot. Kittle may have the job full-time this season, though he's not happy about it.

To solve the 3B hole, look for Russ Morman, a former first sacker, to get a shot. The Sox may also use Darryl Boston (.228) in center in relief of Rudy Law (.259), though Boston may not be ready yet. Bet on young Ozzie Guillen to be at short in 1986 (and, maybe, 1996, too). Guillen, a one-time Padre farmhand, hit .273 as a rookie and made only 12 errors (several for missing 2B on double plays), the best in the majors. 1B Greg Walker (.258) may have to be dealt. OF Harold Baines (.309, fifth in the AL) is here to stay.

Pitching is questionable. Tom Seaver (16–11, a 300-game winner) apparently wants to go home to the East, and Britt Burns (18–11) was dealt to the Yanks for Joe Cowley (12–6). The bullpen, led by Bob James (8–7, 32 saves), is in decent shape. Ex-Ranger Dave Schmidt will also help. A real turnaround situation here.

STAT LEADERS — 1985

BATTING
Average: Baines, .309
Runs: Baines, 86
Hits: Baines, 198
Doubles: Walker, 38
Triples: Guillen, 9
Home Runs: Fisk, 37
RBIs: Baines, 113
Game-Winning RBIs: Baines, 13
Stolen Bases: Law, 29

PITCHING
Wins: Burns, 18
Losses: Bannister, 14
Complete Games: Burns, 8
Shutouts: Burns, 4
Saves: James, 32
Walks: Bannister, 100
Strikeouts: Bannister, 198

AL West
KANSAS CITY ROYALS
1985 Finish: First
1986 Prediction: Third

Willie Wilson　　　　　　　　　　**Frank White**

Just when you think you have the Royals put away, they jump right back at you. The Blue Jays and the Cardinals found out what the AL West teams already knew: Kaycee keeps scrapping until they get you.

Under scrappy manager Dick Howser, that should continue in '86. Not that there isn't room for improvement. Despite SS Buddy Biancalana's postseason heroics, the Royals could do better than Buddy (.188) and Onix Concepcion (.204). The rest of the infield is just fine, thank you. There's plenty of power from 1B Steve Balboni (.243 and 36 homers). 2B Frank White (.249) must improve at the plate, but remains a major plus. 3B George Brett (.335, 112 RBIs, 30 homers) is in a class by himself.

There's a need for more power from the

outfielders. But you can't argue with CF Willie Wilson (.278, 21 triples, 43 steals). The right-field platoon of Pat Sheridan (.228) and Darryl Motley (.222) could be better. Lonnie Smith (.257) is solid in left. Star DH Hal McRae re-signed with Kaycee.

C Jim Sundberg (.245) is a key behind the plate, but could use some support. Pitching, on the other hand, is in great shape, especially if Dennis Leonard bounces back from a season off.

Everyone now knows Cy Young winner Bret Saberhagen (20-6, 2.87), the World Series hero. There's plenty of strength, too, with Charlie Leibrandt (17-9, 2.69), Danny Jackson (14-12, 3.42), Bud Black (10-15, 4.33), and Mark Gubicza (14-10, 4.06). The bullpen, led by all-timer Dan Quisenberry (8-9, 2.37, 37 saves), is in excellent shape.

How can Kaycee repeat? Keep up the mound work, improve the team batting average (a sorry .251), and get some power.

STAT LEADERS — 1985

BATTING
Average: Brett, .335
Runs: Brett, 108
Hits: Brett, 184
Doubles: Brett, 38
Triples: Wilson, 21*
Home Runs: Balboni, 36
RBIs: Brett, 112
Game-Winning RBIs: Brett, 16
Stolen Bases: Wilson, 43

*Led league.

PITCHING
Wins: Saberhagen, 20
Losses: Black, 15
Complete Games: Saberhagen, 10
Shutouts: Leibrandt, Jackson, 3
Saves: Quisenberry, 37*
Walks: Gubicza, 77
Strikeouts: Saberhagen, 158

AL West
MINNESOTA TWINS
1985 Finish: Fourth (tied)
1986 Prediction: Fourth

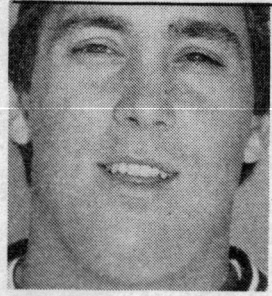
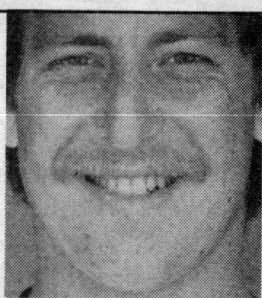

Kent Hrbek   **Frank Viola**

Manager Ray Miller, who saw plenty of success with the Baltimore Orioles, may get some more in the Humphreydome, where the Twins are growing up nicely.

Ray's a pitcher's manager, and he has plenty to start with in Minny. How about Bert Blyleven, late of Cleveland? He led the AL in complete games (24), shutouts (5), and strikeouts (206) last year — at age 34! Now, at 35, he leads the young Twins' staff, including lefty Frank Viola (18–14), Mike Smithson (15–14), and John Butcher (11–14). Ron Davis (only 2–6, but with 25 saves) continues to be the main man in the bullpen. Farmhand Dennis Burtt has a shot at making the staff, which finished 11th in the league in ERA a year ago.

The Twins' defense, in general, is first-rate. And the offense (6th in the AL in batting in '85) isn't bad, either. With an extra year of experience under their belts, they could become a real force in '86.

That will require improved consistency from 1B Kent Hrbek (.278, 93 RBIs). 3B Gary Gaetti hit 20 homers (up from only 5), but slipped in average (.246) and RBIs (64). Rookie Scott Ullger may get a shot here.

Another youngster, Houston Jimenez, will get another chance at shortstop. Steve Lombardozzi may replace Tim Teufel (.260) at second, based on his great glove-work.

RF Tom Brunansky will be back after a quick '85 start but only a .242 finish. CF Kirby Puckett (.288) is set in center.

Miller will rely on C Mark Salas, off his .300 average in 120 games. But Mark needs backup help, and the Twins will be looking for a shortstop, a designated hitter, and a pitcher or two.

STAT LEADERS — 1985

BATTING
Average: Salas, .300
Runs: Puckett, 80
Hits: Puckett, 199
Doubles: Puckett, 29
Triples: Puckett, 29
Home Runs: Brunansky, 27
RBIs: Hrbek, 93
Game-Winning RBIs: Brunansky, 10
Stolen Bases: Puckett, 21

PITCHING*
Wins: Viola, 18
Losses: Blyleven, 16
Complete Games:
    Blyleven, 24**
Shutouts: Blyleven, 5**
Saves: Davis, 25
Walks: Smithson, 78
Strikeouts: Blyleven, 206**

*Blyleven achieved most of his 1985 numbers with Cleveland.
**Led league.

AL West
SEATTLE MARINERS
1985 Finish: Sixth
1986 Prediction: Fifth

Alvin Davis

Mike Moore

The Mariner fans' patience may soon be rewarded. It may not happen in 1986, but it will happen. This ball club will win — and sooner than you might think.

All of which should please manager Chuck Cottier. He has a solid nucleus to build with and may be just a couple of pitchers and possibly a catcher away. Ex-Dodger catcher Steve Yeager, obtained for pitcher Ed Vande Berg, may or may not be the answer.

Here's the good news. OF Phil Bradley (.300 and 26 homers, after never hitting a major-league homer before) is now among the AL's best. 1B Alvin Davis (.287, 78 RBIs) is developing great consistency. (But with little other lefty power available, he sees too few drivable pitches.) 3B Jim Presley (.275,

28 homers) had a fine year, as did OF Al Cowens (.265, 69 RBIs). DH Gorman Thomas (.215, but 32 homers) provides great power.

Look for Danny Tartabull, who smashed a league-leading 43 homers at Calgary of the Pacific Coast League, to get a real shot at shortstop, and there are tons of good young outfielders in the Seattle system, including Ivan Calderon, Rickey Nelson, Al Chambers, and Mickey Brantley. There will be some trades involving Seattle outfielders.

C Bob Kearney, owner of a fairly good arm and a .243 average, needs help. The mound staff, on the other hand, has a great future. Despite a 4.68 team ERA in '85, we like the looks of Matt Young (12-19, 4.91), Mike Moore (17-10, 14 complete games), Mark Langston (7-14), and Billy Swift (6-10).

There's dependable relief help from Edwin Nunez (7-3, 3.09, 16 saves). There could be joy under the Kingdome — soon.

STAT LEADERS — 1985

BATTING
Average: Bradley, .300
Runs: Bradley, 100
Hits: Bradley, 192
Doubles: Bradley,
  Davis, Presley, 33
Home Runs: Thomas, 32
RBIs: Bradley, 88
Game-Winning RBIs: Bradley, 12
Stolen Bases: Perconte, 31

PITCHING
Wins: Moore, 17
Losses: Young, 19*
Complete Games:
  Moore, 14
Shutouts: Moore, Young, 2
Saves: Nunez, 16
Walks: Langston, 91
Strikeouts: Moore, 155

*Led league.

AL West
OAKLAND A's
1985 Finish: Fourth (tied)
1986 Prediction: Sixth

Bruce Bochte

Chris Codiroli

Manager Jackie Moore starts the '86 season with a new one-year contract — and some ongoing problems.

It's nothing that can't be turned around, of course. But there are still some questions to be answered before the A's can become a real contender.

The starting lineup has lots to recommend. There are stick-outs all over the place, possibly led by SS Alfredo Griffin (.270 in all 162 games). He's among the AL's best at the position. 3B Carney Lansford (.277) is a proven hitter, though there were winter trade rumors involving him. CF Dwayne Murphy (.233) was also mentioned in the trade mart.

The A's also had problems on the free-agent front. 1B Bruce Bochte (.295), their leading full-time hitter, was eligible for free-agent status, as was SS Rob Picciolo (.275). Another free agent, P Steve McCatty (4–4) was allowed to leave. And OF Dave Collins (.251) was re-signed and then traded to Detroit for utility player Barbaro Garbey.

Pitching is in worse shape. The relief chiefs, Steve Ontiveros (1–3, 1.93, 8 saves) and Jay Howell (9–8, 2.85, 29 saves), were outstanding, thus atoning for the sins of the starters.

The front-liners, such as José Rijo (6–4), Steve Birtsas (10–6), and Chris Codiroli (14–14, 4 complete games), need backup help. If ex-Card Joaquin Andujar can approach his early '85 performance, the A's could be tough. The price? C Mike Heath.

Among the newcomers, José Canseco, who banged 36 homers at Tacoma (Pacific Coast League) last year, should start in left. Eric Plunk could win a spot in the Oakland pitching rotation. A couple of live arms and better catching will help.

STAT LEADERS — 1985

BATTING
Average: Bochte, .295
Runs: Davis, 92
Hits: Griffin, 166
Doubles: Davis, 34
Triples: Heath, 6
Home Runs: Davis, 24
RBIs: Davis, 82
Game-Winning RBIs: Kingman, 9
Stolen Bases: Collins, 29

PITCHING
Wins: Codiroli, 14
Losses: Codiroli, 14
Complete Games:
  Codiroli, 4
Shutouts: None
Saves: Howell, 29
Walks: Birtsas, 91
Strikeouts: Codiroli, 111

AL West
TEXAS RANGERS
1985 Finish: Seventh
1986 Prediction: Seventh

Gary Ward

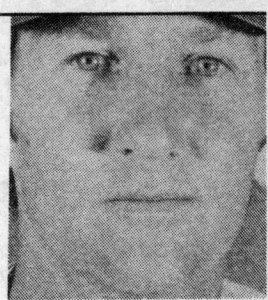
Charlie Hough

We like Bobby Valentine. We believe he's a super baseball man who will make a great manager someday. But not with this bunch in Texas.

Valentine must have been shocked, after leaving the pitching-rich Mets (where he coached) to arrive in Texas and find the mound virtually bare. The Rangers were 12th in the AL in team ERA (4.56), but without Charlie Hough (14–16, 3.31) it could have been much worse. Veteran lefty Mike Mason (8–15, 4.83) lost his spot in the rotation for a while before regaining it late. Greg Harris (5–4, 2.47) leads the bullpen. Dave Schmidt (7–6, 3.15) was traded. Valentine likes youngsters Bobby Witt and Mitch Williams as future Ranger mound stars.

Injuries have hurt the Ranger effort elsewhere on the roster. SS Jeff Kunkel (.250 in two games) underwent knee surgery. Stickout 3B Larry Parrish (.249) missed two months last season.

Everyone was after Ranger 1B Pete O'Brien (.267, 22 homers, 92 RBIs), but he is a Ranger untouchable. So is OF Oddibe McDowell (.239, with loads of ability for the future). There is some other talent, too, including OF Gary Ward (.287) and C Don Slaught (.280). Much-traveled ex-Met Tom Paciorek is a professional hitter.

But SS Alan Bannister (.262) was ready to go the free-agent route, and ex-Expo farmhand and top draftee Pete Incaviglia, a former college home-run king, may be a year away.

Look for Steve Buechele to get a shot at the third-base job and José Guzman to fit into the starting rotation, with vet Ellis Valentine playing somewhere most of the time. The other Valentine, manager Bobby, has plenty of work to do.

STAT LEADERS — 1985

BATTING
Average: Ward, .287
Runs: Ward, 77
Hits: Ward, 170
Doubles: O'Brien, 34
Triples: Ward, 7
Home Runs: O'Brien, 22
RBIs: O'Brien, 92
Game-Winning RBIs: O'Brien, 10
Stolen Bases: Ward, 26

PITCHING
Wins: Hough, 14
Losses: Hough, 16
Complete Games: Hough, 14
Shutouts: Three with 1
Saves: Harris, 11
Walks: Hough, 83
Strikeouts: Hough, 141

What's an Orel Hershiser? To the Dodgers, he's a leader of a super mound staff; to Dodger enemies, he's pure poison.

National League TEAM PREVIEWS

NL East
NEW YORK METS
1985 Finish: Second
1986 Prediction: First

Darryl Strawberry

Ron Darling

The Mets, owners of the NL's best record over the past two seasons but with nothing to show for it, seem poised to finally move to the top in '86.

Manager Davey Johnson is blessed with the league's top pitcher, catcher, and first sacker, with strength sprinkled through the rest of his lineup.

There simply isn't a better hurler on earth than Dwight Gooden (24–4, 1.53 ERA). The rest of the rotation, including Ron Darling (16–6, 2.90), Sid Fernandez (9–9, 2.80 ERA, 180 strikeouts in 170 innings), and Rick Aguilera (10–7), is outstanding. A healthy Ed Lynch (10–8) would help, as will lefty Bob Ojeda (9–11), obtained from the Red Sox. He could start, or join Jesse Orosco (8–6, 17 saves) and Roger McDowell (6–5, 17 saves) in the bullpen. C Gary Carter (.281, 32 homers, 100 RBIs) is the NL's best.

First-sacker Keith Hernandez (a fast-closing .309) has no peer in the NL. His 24 game-winning RBIs set a major-league record in that new stat category. 2B Wally Backman (.273) is more than adequate, though his switch-hitting days may be over. SS Rafael Santana (.257) is an outstanding gloveman, and Johnson is happy (but not thrilled) with his 3B platoon of Howard Johnson (.242 and no relation to the manager) and Ray (husband of golfer Nancy Lopez) Knight (.218).

In the outfield, a healthy Darryl Strawberry (.277, 29 homers, 79 RBIs), who missed seven weeks, might have meant winning the '85 flag. Either Mookie Wilson (.276 and a twice-operated-on shoulder) or peppy Len Dykstra (.254) could be dealt. LF George Foster (.263, 77 RBIs) has had it. Watch for Billy Beane to get a real shot this time.

STAT LEADERS — 1985

BATTING
Average: Hernandez, .309
Runs: Hernandez, 87
Hits: Hernandez, 183
Doubles: Hernandez, 34
Triples: Wilson, 8
Home Runs: Carter, 32
RBIs: Carter, 100
Game-Winning RBIs: Hernandez, 24*
Stolen Bases: Backman, 30

PITCHING
Wins: Gooden, 24*
Losses: Fernandez, 9
Complete Games: Gooden, 16*
Shutouts: Gooden, 8
Saves: Orosco, McDowell, 17
Walks: Darling, 114
Strikeouts: Gooden, 268*

*Led league.

NL East
MONTREAL EXPOS
1985 Finish: Third
1986 Prediction: Second

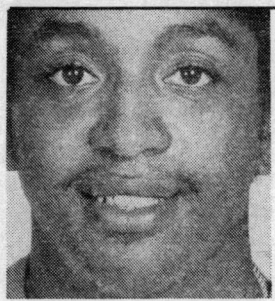
Hubie Brooks

Tim Raines

A healthy pitching staff could make the upcoming season a pleasant one for Montreal manager Buck Rodgers. The Expo skipper, signed through 1987, has plenty of talent and just a few question marks.

Late-season injuries to right-hander David Palmer (7–10), lefty Dan Schatzeder (3-5), and rookie-flash lefty Joe Hesketh (10-5, 2.49 ERA) killed whatever chances Montreal had of catching the front-running Cards and Mets.

Rodgers did have the luxury of the NL's top reliever, one-time Met Jeff Reardon (2–8, but a league-leading 41 saves). The rest of the staff, including young righty Bryn Smith (18–5, 2.91), stick-out rookie reliever Tim Burke (9–4, 2.39 in 78 appearances), and Bill Laskey (5-16) is excellent. The big question? Can Charlie Lea, 15–10 in 1984, make it back from the injuries that kept him out all of '85?

The infield is mostly solid. Ex-Met Hubie Brooks (.269) made the move to shortstop fairly easily, and knocked in 100 runs, most by a NL shortstop since Ernie Banks' 117 in 1960. 2B Vance Law (.266) enjoyed an outstanding season, thus assuring Montreal's strength up the middle. 3B Tim Wallach (.260, 81 RBIs, 22 homers) has stepped to the head of the class among NL third sackers. There is a potential problem at first. Terry Francona (.267) got the full-time job when Dan Driessen was dealt at midseason. But he's unhappy about possibly platooning with Andres Galarraga (.187).

C Mike Fitzgerald (.207, with a poor record of throwing out base stealers) should bounce back from knee surgery. LF Tim Raines (.320, 70 steals, 13 triples) is outstanding, as is RF Andre Dawson (.255, 23 homers), though Dawson could be dealt. Righty pitcher John Dopson could help.

STAT LEADERS — 1985

BATTING
Average: Raines, .320
Runs: Raines, 115
Hits: Raines, 184
Doubles: Wallach, 36
Triples: Raines, 13
Home Runs: Dawson, 23
RBIs: Brooks, 100
Game-Winning RBIs: Brooks, 13
Stolen Bases: Raines, 70

PITCHING
Wins: Smith, 18
Losses: Laskey, 16
Complete Games: Smith, Gullickson, 4
Shutouts: Smith, 2
Saves: Reardon, 41*
Walks: Palmer, 67
Strikeouts: Smith, 127

*Led league.

NL East
ST. LOUIS CARDINALS
1985 Finish: First
1986 Prediction: Third

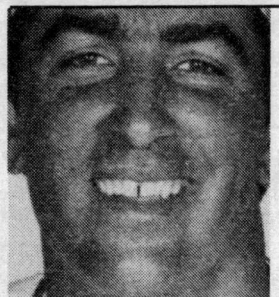

Jack Clark   **Ozzie Smith**

Manager Whitey Herzog's Cardinals did what they had to do to capture the NL title and come within a whisker (and a disputed call) of taking the whole ball of wax in '85. Their 1985 performances gave new meaning to the title of an old movie, *The Best Years of Our Lives*. Whether lightning can strike again in '86 is the key to the Cards' season.

Example: CF Willie McGee, a lifetime .290 hitter with a career high of .296, hit .353, the best ever by an NL switch-hitter. He had his all-time bests in hits (216), runs (114), doubles (26), triples (18), homers (10), RBIs (82), and stolen bases (56). Can he do it again? What about outfield mate Vince Coleman? Can he bounce back from his battle of the tarp and duplicate his leadoff heroics (.267; 107 runs; and 110 stolen bases, the third-best performance ever)? A more-experienced Andy Van Slyke (.259) returns in right.

A healthy 1B Jack Clark (.281, 22 homers) is the power man in the lineup. But can the Cards expect a repeat from 2B Tommy Herr (.302, 110 RBIs), a lifetime .276 hitter who never knocked in more than 49 runs in a season before magical 1985? Herzog can count, however, on his wizard shortshop, Ozzie Smith (.276), who had never hit more than .260 before; and 3B Terry Pendleton (.240) has more experience now.

The NL's top lefty, John Tudor, might be ready to approach his amazing 21-8, 1.93 ERA season. Problem-child Joaquin Andujar (21-12, 3.40) is gone. Danny Cox (18-9, 2.88) and Kurt Kepshire (10-9, 4.75) complete a deep staff, and the bullpen committee (Jeff Lahti, Ken Dayley, and Todd Worrell) is good and deep. Ex-A Mike Heath should handle the catching, with backup help from versatile ex-Met Clint Hurdle.

STAT LEADERS — 1985

BATTING
Average: McGee, .353*
Runs: McGee, 114
Hits: McGee, 216*
Doubles: Herr, 38
Triples: McGee, 18*
Home Runs: Clark, 22
RBIs: Herr, 110
Game-Winning RBIs: McGee, 17
Stolen Bases: Coleman, 110*

PITCHING
Wins: Tudor, Andujar, 21
Losses: Andujar, 12
Complete Games: Tudor, 14
Shutouts: Tudor, 10*
Saves: Lahti, 19
Walks: Andujar, 82
Strikeouts: Tudor, 169

*Led league.

NL East
PHILADELPHIA PHILLIES
1985 Finish: Fifth
1986 Prediction: Fourth

Mike Schmidt

Glenn Wilson

The most common chant heard in Veterans Stadium last summer was: "Strike three!" The Phils led the NL in striking out, which helped seal their doom in the Eastern Division race.

Things should get better for young manager John Felske this summer. For one thing, picking up fleet ex-Red Gary Redus and ex-Brave Milt Thompson firms up the top of the batting order. It also allows Felske to move Von Hayes to 1B and return Mike Schmidt to 3B. Mike shifted to first one third of the way into last year, then rallied to close with 33 homers (his 11th 30-homer season, trailing only Hank Aaron, Babe Ruth, and Jimmie Foxx). The left side of the infield is in great shape, with the surprisingly steady play of SS Tom Foley (.240). 2B Juan Samuel continues to impress, with a .264 average, 13 triples, and 53 steals. But he's also a prime strikeout victim.

In the outfield, Glenn Wilson (.275, 102 RBIs) has risen to among the top NL outfielders. But Jeff Stone (.265) was a flop as a leadoff hitter, pushing the Phils to look for Redus and Thompson. Bonus: Can oft-injured Joe Lefebvre bounce back?

There's concern behind the plate. All-Star Ozzie Virgil slumped from .292 at the midseason break to finish at .246. He's gone to Atlanta. Ex-Brave Steve Bedrosian arrives to help a mound staff hurt by the decline of Lefty Carlton (1–8) and the departures of John Denny (11–14) and Jerry Koosman (6–4).

On the plus side, righty Kevin Gross (15–13) and lefties Don Carman (9–4, 2.08) and Shane Rawley (13–8, 3.31) have developed well. Dave Rucker (3–2) and Dave Shipanoff (8–5, 13 saves) may do it. And ex-Red Tom Hume should strengthen the bullpen.

STAT LEADERS — 1985

BATTING
Average: Schmidt, .277
Runs: Samuel, 101
Hits: Samuel, 175
Doubles: Wilson, 39
Triples: Samuel, 13
Home Runs: Schmidt, 33
RBIs: Wilson, 102
Game-Winning RBIs: Samuel, 13
Stolen Bases: Samuel, 53

PITCHING
Wins: Gross, 15
Losses: Denny, 14
Complete Games: Rawley, Gross, Denny, 6
Shutouts: Rawley, Gross, Denny, 2
Saves: Tekulve, 14
Walks: Denny, 83
Strikeouts: Gross, 151

NL East
CHICAGO CUBS
1985 Finish: Fourth
1986 Prediction: Fifth

Keith Moreland   **Lee Smith**

And the beat goes on. The Cubs, who in 1984 came within a game of winning their first NL pennant since 1945, flopped to the second division in '85. Manager Jim Frey has most of the ingredients he needs to put the pieces together again in '86. But some problems have to be solved before the Cubs have a real shot at the title.

There are at least four absolutely solid citizens in Chi-town. 2B Ryne Sandberg, the hero of the '84 NL East winners, had another outstanding year in '85, hitting .305 with 186 hits and 26 homers. He stole 54 bases. If Tommy Herr slips in St. Louis, Sandberg could return to the top of the NL's second-base corps. C Jody Davis, despite a .232 hit mark and only 58 RBIs (down from 94 in '84), remains one of the league's top backstops. And RF Keith Moreland (.307 and 106 RBIs) will have a spot in the lineup, even if it's at 3B, where he gave it a shot late last season.

3B Ron Cey (.232) flopped at bat and in the field (more than 20 errors) at age 37, raising new questions at that position. SS Shawon Dunston, still projected as a future superstar, must show more than he did in two trials last season.

In the outfield, Moreland may be joined by Thad Bosley (.328 in 180 at-bats), replacing LF Gary Matthews (.235). CF Bob Dernier (.254) has lots of speed.

Healthy pitchers remain the key for manager Frey. Starters Rick Sutcliffe (8–8), Dennis Eckersley (11–7), Steve Trout (9–7), and Scott Sanderson (5–6) all spent time on the disabled list. (They missed 51 starts between 'em.) In all, 18 pitchers won at least one game for the Cubs, with relief ace Lee Smith (7–4, 33 saves) always busy. Righty Jay Baller (2–3) could fit right in.

STAT LEADERS — 1985

BATTING
Average: Moreland, .307
Runs: Sandberg, 113
Hits: Sandberg, 186
Doubles: Durham, 32
Triples: Sandberg, 6
Home Runs: Sandberg, 26
RBIs: Moreland, 106
Game-Winning RBIs: Moreland, 12
Stolen Bases: Sandberg, 54

PITCHING
Wins: Eckersley, 11
Losses: Fontenot, 10
Complete Games:
    Eckersley, Sutcliffe, 6
Shutouts: Sutcliffe, 3
Saves: Smith, 33
Walks: Trout, 63
Strikeouts: Eckersley, 117

NL East
PITTSBURGH PIRATES
1985 Finish: Sixth
1986 Prediction: Sixth

Johnny Ray   **Rick Reuschel**

The Pirates will start the '86 season with lots of new faces, including manager Jim Leyland. But at least they will be in Pittsburgh, thanks to new ownership.

Whether the new bosses will help produce any improvement on the field is doubtful. The Pirates have no untouchables, and any player listed here may be gone by the time the season opens.

The top Bucs are 2B Johnny Ray (.274), whose 70 RBIs led the Bucs, and OF Joe Orsulak, whose .300 average was the best by a Pirate rookie since C Tony Pena in 1981.

The outfield has great potential. Orsulak looks like a winner, and newcomers ex-Angel Mike Brown (.332 in 57 games) and ex-Dodger R.J. Reynolds (.282) should join him.

Though the Pirates are struggling without much team power, the trade with L.A. for long-time bat king Bill Madlock could pay off soon. In addition to Reynolds, the Bucs picked up SS Cecil Espy and 1B Sid Bream, both of whom could help rebuild this club. Young Sammy Khalifa (.238 in 95 games) is solid defensively but powerless at the plate. 3B Denny Gonzalez (.226) could be a future star because of power potential.

Some experts raised eyebrows when the Bucs gave comeback pitcher Rick Reuschel (14–8, 2.27 ERA) a new three-year pact at age 36. Vet Rick Rhoden (10–15) asked to be traded (though he could not demand one). José DeLeon, the team's strikeout leader, went 2–19, much of it in hard-luck situations.

Lefty Larry McWilliams (7–9) could be shifted to the bullpen, along with rookie righty Barry Jones. Lefty Bob Kipper could be a real Buc find, though he was being mentioned in trade talks. Still, there are too many holes on this club.

STAT LEADERS — 1985

BATTING
Average: Orsulak, .300
Runs: Ray, 67
Hits: Ray, 163
Doubles: Ray, 33
Triples: Reynolds, 7
Home Runs: Thompson, 12
RBIs: Ray, 70
Game-Winning RBIs: Reynolds, 8
Stolen Bases: Orsulak, 24

PITCHING
Wins: Reuschel, 14
Losses: DeLeon, 19*
Complete Games: Reuschel, 9
Shutouts: Reuschel, Walk, 1
Saves: Candelaria, 9
Walks: DeLeon, 89
Strikeouts: DeLeon, 149

*Led league.

NL West
LOS ANGELES DODGERS
1985 Finish: First
1986 Prediction: First

Mike Scioscia **Orel Hershiser**

Tommy (Dodger Blue) Lasorda is set in the manager's office until 1988. With that security in his pocket, he can turn his attention to the field, where the picture is also secure.

LA arrived at spring training, unlike most clubs, all set for opening day. The acquisition of ex-Pirate bat king Bill Madlock (.275) solved Lasorda's problems at 3B. The instant stardom for Mariano Duncan (.244) at SS has eliminated another Dodger hole. Steve Sax (.279), his scatter-arm under control, is set at second, with much-improved Greg Brock (.251, 66 RBIs) ready to go at 1B. The Dodger infield opened the '85 season as one of the NL's worst; they were in far better shape at the end.

In the outfield, Pedro Guerrero's full-time

return, complete with .320 average and 33 homers, provides great strength. In-and-out Mike Marshall (.293, 28 homers, 95 RBIs) has a lot more ins than outs these days. Look for several farmhands, including Ralph Bryant, José Gonzalez, and Franklin Stubbs, to get a real shot at making the big club.

Mike Scioscia (.296, but only 52 RBIs) has become one of the NL's best catchers. With vet Steve Yeager gone to Seattle for P Ed Vande Berg, rookie Gilberto Reyes or journeyman Alex Trevino could be the backup.

Starting pitching is wonderful, with youngsters like lefty ace Fernando Valenzuela (17–10, 2.45), Orel Hershiser (a sparkling 19–3 and 2.03), and Bob Welch (14–4, 2.31). If Alejandro Pena, who pitched only twice in '85, bounces back, LA might even improve its league-leading 2.96 ERA. The bullpen, featuring Tom Niedenfuer (19 saves), Ken Howell (12 saves), and Vande Berg is fine. Improved defense could help the Dodgers dominate in '86.

STAT LEADERS — 1985

BATTING
Average: Guerrero, .320
Runs: Guerrero, 99
Hits: Guerrero, 156
Doubles: Marshall, 27
Triples: Duncan, 6
Home Runs: Guerrero, 33
RBIs: Marshall, 95
Game-Winning RBIs: Guerrero, 16
Stolen Bases: Duncan, 38

PITCHING
Wins: Hershiser, 19
Losses: Honeycutt, 12
Complete Games: Valenzuela, 14
Shutouts: Hershiser, Valenzuela, 5
Saves: Niedenfuer, 19
Walks: Valenzuela, 101
Strikeouts: Valenzuela, 208

NL West
SAN DIEGO PADRES
1985 Finish: Third (tied)
1986 Prediction: Second

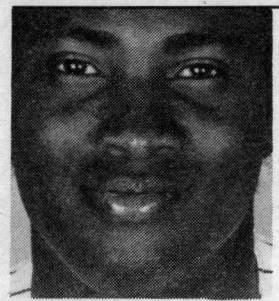

Tony Gwynn **Goose Gossage**

It's a short drop from the penthouse to the basement, as Padre manager Dick Williams learned a year ago. Not that his club finished anywhere near the NL West basement. But San Diego did fall from a perch, five games ahead of the pack, in July, down to a final tie for third, 12 games off the pace. That means new, intense pressure on the veteran skipper.

The situation can be rescued, however. The team has strength in a lot of key areas, most notably in the outfield, where Tony Gwynn (.317) had a second straight dynamite year — not like his .351 '84 season, when he won the NL hit crown, but nothing to be ashamed of. A healthy SS Garry Templeton (he had surgery late in the season) should duplicate his .282 mark and stellar fielding. And there's great strength in the bullpen, where Goose Gossage (5–3, 26 saves, 1.82 ERA) now has help in long and short relief from Gene Walter and Lance McCullers.

There are shortcomings. The outfield, aside from Gwynn, isn't much to write home about defensively. Carmelo Martinez (.253, 21 homers) can hit, and Kevin McReynolds (.234) can improve. Martinez may get a shot at 3B, where vet star Graig Nettles (.261) will reach age 42 this season. Outfield help could come from the Pacific Coast League's two top hitters, John Kruk (.351) and Rusty Tillman (.337). C Terry Kennedy (.261) will be pushed by Ray Smith, James Steels, and, coming soon, Benito Santiago.

Starting pitching is in decent shape, with Dave Dravecky (13–11), Andy Hawkins (18–8), Mark Thurmond (7–11), and getting-slimmer-all-the-time LaMarr Hoyt (16–8). Eric Show (12–11) isn't the most popular Padre.

STAT LEADERS — 1985

BATTING
Average: Gwynn, .317
Runs: Gwynn, 90
Hits: Gwynn, 197
Doubles: Garvey, 34
Triples: Garvey, 6
Home Runs: Martinez, 21
RBIs: Garvey, 81
Game-Winning RBIs: Martinez, 13
Stolen Bases: Dilone, 17

PITCHING
Wins: Hawkins, 18
Losses: Dravecky, Show, Thurmond, 11
Complete Games: Hoyt, 8
Shutouts: Hoyt, 3
Saves: Gossage, 26
Walks: Show, 87
Strikeouts: Show, 141

NL West
CINCINNATI REDS
1985 Finish: Second
1986 Prediction: Third

 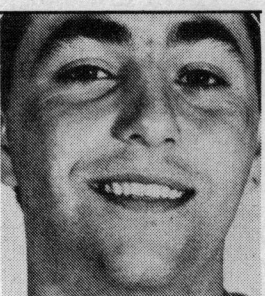

Dave Parker **John Franco**

The experts predicted that Cincinnati would finish in Ohio a year ago. Nothing fancy. No one ever dreamed that washed-up Dave Parker would enjoy the best year of his life, that player Pete Rose could still hit .264, and that manager Pete Rose could — well — manage.

Still, Charlie Hustle wasn't satisfied with his team's second-place finish in '85, and he has his sights set on the '86 flag. We don't think so.

Buddy Bell (.219) must improve with the bat to become one of the league's leading third sackers. And 37-year-old SS Dave Concepcion (.252) will have to become more consistent to keep 20-year-old Kurt Stillwell out of the lineup. 2B Ron Oester (.295) is a solid citizen of the Cincy infield, with Rose and (perhaps) Tony Perez (.328 in 72 games) ready to return at first. Perez will turn 44 in May. Wayne Krenchicki (.272), who lost his 3B job to Bell, is ready to fill in anywhere.

Parker (.312, 34 homers, 125 RBIs, 42 doubles) is the key to the outfield. OF Gary Redus is off to Philly, but youngsters Eric Davis, Paul O'Neill, and Kal Daniels (the latter off a great American Association season) are ready to step in.

Midseason pickup Bo Diaz, like Bell, will have to hit better than in '85.

Tom Browning (20–9), the NL's first rookie 20-game winner in 32 years, was Cincy's only consistent starter in '85. Strikeout artist Mario Soto (12–15) and ex-Phil Cy Young winner John Denny must bounce back, along with in-and-out Jay Tibbs (10–16). A return to health by Joe Price and Frank Pastore would help. The bullpen, led by powerful Ted Power (8–6, 27 saves) and John Franco (12–2, 12 saves), is in great shape.

STAT LEADERS — 1985

BATTING
Average: Parker, .312
Runs: Parker, 88
Hits: Parker, 198
Doubles: Parker, 42*
Triples: Milner, 7
Home Runs: Parker, 34
RBIs: Parker, 125*
Game-Winning RBIs: Parker, 18
Stolen Bases: Redus, 48

PITCHING
Wins: Browning, 20
Losses: Tibbs, 16
Complete Games: Soto, 9
Shutouts: Browning, 4
Saves: Power, 27
Walks: Soto, 104
Strikeouts: Soto, 214

*Led league.

NL West
HOUSTON ASTROS
1985 Finish: Third (tied)
1986 Prediction: Fourth

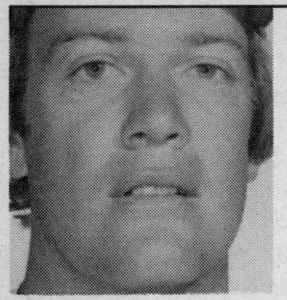 

Mike Scott   **Bill Doran**

One of the Astros' goals in 1985 was to improve team power. They moved in the outfield fences and the number of Astrodome home runs doubled.

Now, under new manager Hal Lanier, the Astros' goals for '86 include improved pitching and improved speed. They can't move the mound or widen the plate, and they can't shorten the basepaths. This will take a little more effort.

In obtaining Hal Lanier, former Cardinal coach, to be the manager, Houston management hopes to install some of the tactics that led the Redbirds to the 1985 NL flag. There are possibilities.

2B Bill Doran (.287, 23 steals) continues to do an outstanding job. The team's 1985 most valuable player had appendix surgery during the off-season but should be ready in the spring. At age 38, OF José Cruz continues to bash the ball with authority, as his .300 average and 79 RBIs in '85 prove. And young Glenn Davis, who led the Astros in homers (20) despite only 350 at-bats following a June 13 arrival from the minors, could be a real find.

There's some strength on the mound, too, like one-time Met Mike Scott (18–8, 3.29) and Bob Knepper (15–13, 3.55).

But there are serious pitching problems, particularly in long relief, including a whopping total of 543 walks allowed. Look for Charlie Kerfeld (4–2), who ended the season with 14 scoreless innings, and Jeff Heathcock (3–1) to get real shots in '86. Reliever Bill Dawley (5–3) should bounce back from bone chip problems.

Aging (36) Phil Garner will probably be back at third base, with 34-year-old catcher Alan Ashby back to support catcher Mark Bailey (.265).

STAT LEADERS — 1985

BATTING
Average: Cruz, .300
Runs: Doran, 84
Hits: Doran, 166
Doubles: Cruz, 34
Triples: Garner, 10
Home Runs: Davis, 20
RBIs: Cruz, 79
Game-Winning RBIs: Cruz, 9
Stolen Bases: Doran, 23

PITCHING
Wins: Scott, 18
Losses: Knepper, 13
Complete Games:
   Four with 4
Shutouts: Scott, 2
Saves: Smith, 27
Walks: Niekro, 99
Strikeouts: Ryan, 209

NL West
ATLANTA BRAVES
1985 Finish: Fifth
1986 Prediction: Fifth

Bob Horner **Rick Mahler**

Hard to believe that a team featuring Dale Murphy and Bob Horner batting back-to-back could lose 96 games and finish 29 games off the pennant pace. But a check of the NL stats, which show the Braves 10th in batting (.246) and last in pitching (4.19), tells you why Ted Turner cleaned the entire house last fall.

New manager Chuck Tanner, who has been successful everywhere he has gone, and new general manager Bobby Cox, last year's AL Manager of the Year, will likely have a free hand to reshape the club into the contenders Turner thinks they should be.

Horner, who missed 32 games a year ago, should open at 1B. His .267 mark, with 27 homers and 89 RBIs can only improve over a full, healthy season. Little Glenn Hubbard (.232) must regain his batting touch, and SS Rafael Ramirez (.248), who slumped late in '85, had better start quickly because rookie Andres Thomas (.278 in 15 late-season games) is breathing down his neck. Atlanta re-signed free agent Ken Oberkfell (.272), who should return at 3B.

The outfield is anchored by Murphy (.300, 37 homers, 111 RBIs), the NL's year-in, year-out homer king. RF Claudell Washington (.276) signed a new one-year contract, but Milt Thompson (.302 in 73 games) and Terry Harper (.264) should see most of the action with Murphy.

C Bruce Benedict (.202) got a new three-year pact, but the Braves picked up ex-Phil C Ozzie Virgil, a far better hitter (with power), for P Steve Bedrosian. Watch for another trade here.

A healthy Len Barker (2–9) and Pascual Perez (1–13) would help, of course. But Tanner will have to rely on Rick Mahler (17–15).

STAT LEADERS — 1985

BATTING
Average: Murphy, .300
Runs: Murphy, 118*
Hits: Murphy, 185
Doubles: Murphy, 32
Triples: Washington, 6
Home Runs: Murphy, 37*
RBIs: Murphy, 111
Game-Winning RBIs: Murphy, 14
Stolen Bases: Washington, 14

PITCHING
Wins: Mahler, 17
Losses: Mahler, Bedrosian, 15
Complete Games: Mahler, 6
Shutouts: Smith, 2
Saves: Sutter, 23
Walks: Bedrosian, 111
Strikeouts: Bedrosian, 134

*Led league.

NL West
SAN FRANCISCO GIANTS
1985 Finish: Sixth
1986 Prediction: Sixth

Chili Davis **Scott Garrelts**

It's hard to make predictions on the Giants. Fact is, at press time, it was impossible to predict where they'd be playing in 1986. After the '85 season, when owner Bob Lurie declared, "The Giants will never again play in Candlestick Park," he set off a barrage of meetings, votes, and rumors, creating new interest in the club — despite the worst season in the history of the team (100 losses).

Would they play in Oakland? Would they play in Denver? Would they play in Washington? Would they, in fact, play in Candlestick? Under this kind of cloud, new GM Al Rosen and new manager Roger Craig tried to rebuild the ball club so badly in need of rebuilding.

To be sure, it's not an impossible task. It

just looks that way. The Giants have very few players anyone else really wants. The left side of the infield isn't bad at all. Most clubs would like to have 24-year-old 3B Chris Brown (.271) and SS José Uribe (.237). 1B Dan Driessen (.243) has enjoyed big seasons elsewhere and is being counted on to bounce back with the Giants. Mike Woodard, who hit in his first 12 games as a Giant in September, could get a shot at 2B.

The outfield is two-thirds complete with desirable players. Chili Davis (.270) could start for almost anyone, and Dan Gladden (.243) has enjoyed back-to-back 30-steal seasons. Young ex-Dodger Candy Maldonado could complete the trio.

The pitching staff, which started fast, then faded, includes top reliever Scott Garrelts (9–6, 13 saves) with starters like Mike Krukow (8–11), Atlee Hammaker (5–12), and Vida Blue (8–8). C Bob Melvin, obtained from Detroit for Dave LaPoint, could fit right in.

STAT LEADERS — 1985

BATTING
Average: Brown, .271
Runs: Gladden, 64
Hits: Davis, 130
Doubles: Davis, 25
Triples: Gladden, 8
Home Runs: Brenly, 19
RBIs: Leonard, 62
Game-Winning RBIs: Brown, 10
Stolen Bases: Leonard, 32

PITCHING
Wins: Garrelts, 9
Losses: LaPoint, 17
Complete Games: Krukow, 6
Shutouts: Four with 1
Saves: Garrelts, 13
Walks: Blue, 80
Strikeouts: Krukow, 150

For the Royals to repeat, they'll need another super year out of 3B George Brett, the spark that makes 'em go.

STATISTICS
1985

AMERICAN LEAGUE
Batting

(50 or more at-bats)
*Bats Lefthanded †Switch-Hitter

Batter and Club	AVG	G	AB	R	H	HR	RBI	SB
Armas, Tony, Bos.	.265	103	385	50	102	23	64	0
Ayala, Benny, Clev.	.250	46	76	10	19	2	15	0
Baines, Harold, Chi.*	.309	160	640	86	198	22	113	1
Baker, Dusty, Oak.	.268	111	343	48	92	14	52	2
Balboni, Steve, K.C.	.243	160	600	74	146	36	88	1
Bando, Chris, Clev.†	.139	73	173	11	24	0	13	0
Bannister, Alan, Tex.	.262	57	122	17	32	1	6	8
Barfield, Jesse, Tor.	.289	155	539	94	156	27	84	22
Barrett, Marty, Bos	.266	156	534	59	142	5	56	7
Baylor, Don, N.Y.	.231	142	477	70	110	23	91	0
Bell, Buddy, Tex.	.236	84	313	33	74	4	32	3
Bell, George, Tor.	.275	157	607	87	167	28	95	21
Beniquez, Juan, Cal.	.304	132	411	54	125	8	42	4
Benton, Butch, Clev.	.179	31	67	5	12	0	7	0
Bergman, Dave, Det.*	.179	69	140	8	25	3	7	0
Bernazard, Tony, Clev.†	.274	153	500	73	137	11	59	17
Berra, Dale, N.Y.	.229	48	109	8	25	1	8	1
Biancalana, Buddy, K.C.†	.188	81	138	21	26	1	6	1
Bochte, Bruce, Oak.*	.295	137	424	48	125	14	60	3
Boggs, Wade, Bos.*	.368	161	653	107	240	8	78	2
Bonnell, Barry, Sea.	.243	48	111	9	27	1	10	1
Boone, Bob, Cal.	.248	150	460	37	114	5	55	1
Boston, Daryl, Chi.*	.228	95	232	20	53	3	15	8
Bradley, Phil, Sea.	.300	159	641	100	192	26	88	22
Brett, George, K.C.*	.335	155	550	108	184	30	112	9
Brookens, Tom, Det.	.237	156	485	54	115	7	47	14
Brouhard, Mark, Milw.	.259	37	108	11	28	1	13	0
Brown, Mike, Cal.	.268	60	153	23	41	4	20	0
Brummer, Glenn, Tex.	.278	49	108	7	30	0	5	1
Brunansky, Tom, Minn.	.242	157	567	71	137	27	90	5
Buckner, Bill, Bos.*	.299	162	673	89	201	16	110	18

Batter and Club	AVG	G	AB	R	H	HR	RBI	SB
Buechele, Steve, Tex.	.219	69	219	22	48	6	21	3
Burroughs, Jeff, Tor.	.257	86	191	19	49	6	28	0
Bush, Randy, Minn*	.239	97	234	26	56	10	35	3
Butler, Brett, Clev.*	.311	152	591	106	184	5	50	47
Calderon, Ivan, Sea.	.286	67	210	37	60	8	28	4
Canseco, Jose, Oak.	.302	29	96	16	29	5	13	1
Carew, Rod, Cal.*	.280	127	443	69	124	2	39	5
Carter, Joe, Clev.	.262	143	489	64	128	15	59	24
Castillo, Carmen, Clev.	.245	67	184	27	45	11	25	3
Castillo, Marty, Det.	.119	57	84	4	10	2	5	0
Clark, Bobby, Milw.	.226	29	93	6	21	0	8	1
Coles, Darnell, Sea.	.237	27	59	8	14	1	5	0
Collins, Dave, Oak.†	.251	112	379	52	95	4	29	29
Concepcion, Onix, K.C.	.204	131	314	32	64	2	20	4
Connally, Fritz, Balt.	.232	50	112	16	26	3	15	0
Cooper, Cecil, Milw.*	.293	154	631	82	185	16	99	10
Cotto, Henry, N.Y.	.304	34	56	4	17	1	6	1
Cowens, Al, Sea.	.265	122	452	59	120	14	69	0
Cruz, Julio, Chi.†	.197	91	234	28	46	0	15	8
Dauer, Rich, Balt.	.202	85	208	25	42	2	14	0
Davis, Alvin, Sea.*	.287	155	578	78	166	18	78	1
Davis, Mike, Oak.*	.287	154	547	92	157	24	82	24
DeCinces, Doug, Cal.	.244	120	427	50	104	20	78	1
Dempsey, Rick, Balt.	.254	132	362	54	92	12	52	0
Downing, Brian, Cal.	.263	150	520	80	137	20	85	5
Dunbar, Tommy, Tex.*	.202	45	104	7	21	1	5	0
Dwyer, Jim, Balt.*	.249	101	233	35	58	7	36	0
Easler, Mike, Bos.*	.262	155	568	71	149	16	74	0
Engle, Dave, Minn.	.256	70	172	28	44	7	25	2
Espinoza, Alvaro, Minn.	.263	32	57	5	15	0	9	0
Evans, Darrell, Det.*	.248	151	505	81	125	40	94	0
Evans, Dwight, Bos.	.263	159	617	110	162	29	78	7
Felder, Mike, Milw.†	.196	15	56	8	11	0	0	4
Fernandez, Tony, Tor.†	.289	161	564	71	163	2	51	13
Fielder, Cecil, Tor.	.311	30	74	6	23	4	16	0
Fischlin, Mike, Clev.	.200	73	60	12	12	0	2	0
Fisk, Carlton, Chi.	.238	153	543	85	129	37	107	17

Batter and Club	AVG	G	AB	R	H	HR	RBI	SB
Fletcher, Scott, Chi.	.256	119	301	38	77	2	31	5
Flynn, Doug, Det.	.255	32	51	2	13	0	2	0
Ford, Dan, Balt.	.187	28	75	4	14	1	1	0
Franco, Julio, Clev.	.288	160	636	97	183	6	90	13
Funderburk, Mark, Minn.	.314	23	70	7	22	2	13	0
Gaetti, Gary, Minn.	.246	160	560	71	138	20	63	13
Gagne, Greg, Minn.	.225	114	293	37	66	2	23	10
Gallego, Mike, Oak.	.208	76	77	13	16	1	9	1
Gamble, Oscar, Chi.*	.203	70	148	20	30	4	20	0
Gantner, Jim, Milw.*	.254	143	523	63	133	5	44	11
Garbey, Barbaro, Det.	.257	86	237	27	61	6	29	3
Garcia, Damaso, Tor.	.282	146	600	70	169	8	65	28
Gedman, Rich, Bos.*	.295	144	498	66	147	18	80	2
Gerber, Graig, Cal.*	.264	65	91	8	24	0	6	0
Gibson, Kirk, Det.*	.287	154	581	96	167	29	97	30
Giles, Brian, Milw.	.172	34	58	6	10	1	1	2
Grich, Bobby, Cal.	.242	144	479	74	116	13	53	3
Griffey, Ken, N.Y.*	.274	127	438	68	120	10	69	7
Griffin, Alfredo, Oak.†	.270	162	614	75	166	2	64	24
Gross, Wayne, Balt.*	.235	103	217	31	51	11	18	1
Grubb, John, Det.*	.245	78	155	19	38	5	25	0
Guillen, Ozzie, Chi.*	.273	150	491	71	134	1	33	7
Gutierrez, Jackie, Bos.	.218	103	275	33	60	2	21	10
Hairston, Jerry, Chi.†	.243	95	140	9	34	2	20	0
Hall, Mel, Clev.*	.318	23	66	7	21	0	12	0
Hargrove, Mike, Clev.*	.285	107	284	31	81	1	27	1
Harrah, Toby, Tex.	.270	126	396	65	107	9	44	11
Hassey, Ron, N.Y.*	.296	92	267	31	79	13	42	0
Hatcher, Mickey, Minn.	.282	116	444	46	125	3	49	0
Heath, Mike, Oak.	.250	138	436	71	109	13	55	7
Henderson, Dave, Sea.	.241	139	502	70	121	14	68	6
Henderson, Rickey, N.Y.	.314	143	547	146	172	24	72	80
Henderson, Steve, Oak.	.301	85	193	25	58	3	31	0
Herndon, Larry, Det.	.244	137	442	45	108	12	37	2
Hill, Donnie, Oak.†	.285	123	393	45	112	3	48	8
Hill, Marc, Chi.	.133	40	75	5	10	0	4	0
Hoffman, Glenn, Bos.	.276	96	279	40	77	6	34	2

Batter and Club	AVG	G	AB	R	H	HR	RBI	SB
Householder, Paul, Milw.†	.258	95	299	41	77	11	34	1
Howell, Jack, Cal.*	.197	43	137	19	27	5	18	1
Hrbek, Kent, Minn.*	.278	158	593	78	165	21	93	1
Hudler, Rex, N.Y.	.157	20	51	4	8	0	1	0
Hulett, Tim, Chi.	.268	141	395	52	106	5	37	6
Iorg, Dane, K.C.*	.223	64	130	7	29	1	21	0
Iorg, Garth, Tor.	.313	131	288	33	90	7	37	2
Jackson, Reggie, Cal.*	.252	143	460	64	116	27	85	1
Jacoby, Brook, Clev.	.274	161	606	72	166	20	87	2
Johnson, Cliff, Tex.-Tor.	.260	106	369	35	96	13	66	0
Jones, Bobby, Tex.*	.224	83	134	14	30	5	23	1
Jones, Lynn, K.C.	.211	110	152	12	32	0	9	0
Jones, Ruppert, Cal.*	.231	125	389	66	90	21	67	7
Kearney, Bob, Sea.	.243	108	305	24	74	6	27	1
Kiefer, Steve, Oak.	.197	40	66	8	13	1	10	0
Kingman, Dave, Oak.	.238	158	592	66	141	30	91	3
Kittle, Ron, Chi.	.230	116	379	51	87	26	58	1
Lacy, Lee, Balt.	.293	121	492	69	144	9	48	10
Lansford, Carney, Oak.	.277	98	401	51	111	13	46	2
Laudner, Tim, Minn.	.238	72	164	16	39	7	19	0
Law, Rudy, Chi.*	.259	125	390	62	101	4	36	29
Lemon, Chet, Det.	.265	145	517	69	137	18	68	0
Little, Bryan, Chi.†	.250	73	188	35	47	2	27	0
Loman, Doug, Milw.*	.212	24	66	10	14	0	7	0
Lombardozzi, Steve, Minn.	.370	28	54	10	20	0	6	3
Lynn, Fred, Balt.*	.263	124	448	59	118	23	68	7
Lyons, Steve, Bos.*	.264	133	371	52	98	5	30	12
Manning, Rick, Milw.*	.218	79	216	19	47	2	18	1
Martinez, Buck, Tor.	.162	42	99	11	16	4	14	0
Mattingly, Don, N.Y.*	.324	159	652	107	211	35	145	2
Matuszek, Leonard, Tor.*	.212	62	151	23	32	2	15	2
McDowell, Oddibe, Tex.*	.239	111	406	63	97	18	42	25
McRae, Hal, K.C.	.259	112	320	41	83	14	70	0
Meacham, Bobby, N.Y.†	.218	156	481	70	105	1	47	25
Meier, Dave, Minn.	.260	71	104	15	27	1	8	0
Melvin, Bob, Det.	.220	41	82	10	18	0	4	0
Molitor, Paul, Milw.	.297	140	576	93	171	10	48	21

Batter and Club	AVG	G	AB	R	H	HR	RBI	SB
Moore, Charlie, Milw.	.232	105	349	35	81	0	31	4
Moreno, Omar, N.Y.-K.C*	.221	58	136	21	30	3	16	1
Moseby, Lloyd, Tor.*	.259	152	584	92	151	18	70	37
Moses, John, Sea.†	.194	33	62	4	12	0	3	5
Motley, Darryl, K.C.	.222	123	383	45	85	17	49	6
Mulliniks, Rance, Tor.*	.295	129	366	55	108	10	57	2
Murphy, Dwayne, Oak.*	.233	152	523	77	122	20	59	4
Murray, Eddie, Balt.†	.297	156	583	111	173	31	124	5
Narron, Jerry, Cal.*	.220	67	132	12	29	5	14	0
Nichols, Reid, Bos.-Chi.	.273	72	150	23	41	2	18	6
Nixon, Otis, Clev.†	.235	104	162	34	38	3	9	20
O'Brien, Pete, Tex.*	.267	159	573	69	153	22	92	5
Oglivie, Ben, Milw.*	.290	101	341	40	99	10	61	0
Oliver, Al, Tor.*	.251	61	187	20	47	5	23	0
Orta, Jorge, K.C.*	.267	110	300	32	80	4	45	2
Owen, Spike, Sea.†	.259	118	352	41	91	6	37	11
Paciorek, Tom, Chi.	.246	46	122	14	30	0	9	2
Pagliarulo, Mike, N.Y.*	.239	138	380	55	91	19	62	0
Pardo, Al, Balt.†	.133	34	75	3	10	0	1	0
Parrish, Lance, Det.	.273	140	549	64	150	28	98	2
Parrish, Larry, Tex.	.249	94	346	44	86	17	51	0
Pasqua, Dan, N.Y.*	.209	60	148	17	31	9	25	0
Perconte, Jack, Sea.*	.264	125	485	60	128	2	23	31
Petralli, Geno, Tex.†	.270	42	100	7	27	0	11	1
Pettis, Gary, Cal.†	.257	125	443	67	114	1	32	56
Phelps, Ken, Sea.*	.207	61	116	18	24	9	24	2
Phillips, Tony, Oak.†	.280	42	161	23	45	4	17	3
Picciolo, Rob, Oak.	.275	71	102	19	28	1	8	3
Pittaro, Chris, Det.†	.242	28	62	10	15	0	7	1
Ponce, Carlos, Milw.	.161	21	62	4	10	1	5	0
Presley, Jim, Sea	.275	155	570	71	157	28	84	2
Pryor, Greg, K.C.	.219	63	114	8	25	1	3	0
Puckett, Kirby, Minn	.288	161	691	80	199	4	74	21
Quirk, Jamie, K.C.*	.281	19	57	3	16	0	4	0
Ramos, Domingo, Sea	.196	75	168	19	33	1	15	0
Randolph, Willie, N.Y.	.276	143	497	75	137	5	40	16
Rayford, Floyd, Balt	.306	105	359	55	110	18	48	3

Batter and Club	AVG	G	AB	R	H	HR	RBI	SB
Ready, Randy, Milw.	.265	48	181	29	48	1	21	0
Reynolds, Harold, Sea.†	.144	67	104	15	15	0	6	3
Rice, Jim, Bos.	.291	140	546	85	159	27	103	2
Riles, Earnest, Milw.*	.286	116	448	54	128	5	45	2
Ripken, Cal, Balt	.282	161	642	116	181	26	110	2
Robertson, Andre, N.Y.	.328	50	125	16	41	2	17	1
Robidoux, B.J., Milw.*	.176	18	51	5	9	3	8	0
Roenicke, Gary, Balt.	.218	113	225	36	49	15	43	2
Romero, Ed, Milw.	.251	88	251	24	63	0	21	1
Sakata, Lenn, Balt.	.227	55	97	15	22	3	6	3
Salas, Mark, Minn.*	.300	120	360	51	108	9	41	0
Salazar, Luis, Chi.	.245	122	327	39	80	10	45	14
Sample, Billy, N.Y.	.288	59	139	18	40	1	15	2
Sanchez, Alejandro, Det.	.248	71	133	19	33	6	12	2
Schofield, Dick, Cal.	.219	147	438	50	96	8	41	11
Schroeder, Bill, Milw.	.242	53	194	18	47	8	25	0
Sconiers, Daryl, Cal.*	.286	44	98	14	28	2	12	2
Scott, Donnie, Sea.†	.222	80	185	18	41	4	23	1
Sheets, Larry, Balt.*	.262	113	328	43	86	17	50	0
Shelby, John, Balt.†	.283	69	205	28	58	7	27	5
Sheridan, Pat, K.C.*	.228	78	206	18	47	3	17	11
Simmons, Nelson, Det.†	.239	75	251	31	60	10	33	1
Simmons, Ted, Milw.†	.273	143	528	60	144	12	76	1
Slaught, Don, Tex.	.280	102	343	34	96	8	35	5
Smalley, Roy, Minn.†	.258	129	388	57	100	12	45	0
Smith, Lonnie, K.C.	.257	120	448	77	115	6	41	40
Stapleton, Dave, Bos.	.227	30	66	4	15	0	2	0
Stein, Bill, Tex.	.253	44	79	5	20	1	12	0
Stenhouse, Mike, Minn.	.223	81	179	23	40	5	21	1
Sullivan, Marc, Bos.	.174	32	69	10	12	2	3	0
Sundberg, Jim, K.C.	.245	115	367	38	90	10	35	0
Tabler, Pat, Clev.	.275	117	404	47	111	5	59	0
Tartabull, Danny, Sea.	.328	19	61	8	20	1	7	1
Tettleton, Mickey, Oak.†	.251	78	211	23	53	3	15	2
Teufel, Tim, Minn.	.260	138	434	58	113	10	50	4
Thomas, Gorman, Sea.	.215	135	484	76	104	32	87	3
Thornton, Andre, Clev.	.236	124	461	49	109	22	88	3

Batter and Club	AVG	G	AB	R	H	HR	RBI	SB
Thornton, Louis, Tor.*	.236	56	72	18	17	1	8	1
Tolleson, Wayne, Tex.†	.313	123	323	45	101	1	18	21
Trammell, Alan, Det.	.258	149	605	79	156	13	57	14
Upshaw, Willie, Tor.*	.275	148	501	79	138	15	65	8
Valle, Dave, Sea.	.157	31	70	2	11	0	4	0
Vukovich, George, Clev.*	.244	149	434	43	106	8	45	2
Walker, Duane, Tex.*	.174	53	132	14	23	5	11	2
Walker, Greg, Chi.*	.258	163	601	77	155	24	92	5
Ward, Gary, Tex.	.287	154	593	77	150	15	70	26
Washington, Ron, Minn.	.274	70	135	24	37	1	14	5
Wathan, John, K.C.	.234	60	145	11	34	1	9	1
Whitaker, Lou, Det.*	.279	152	609	102	170	21	73	6
White, Frank, K.C.	.249	149	563	62	140	22	69	10
Whitt, Ernie, Tor.*	.245	139	412	55	101	19	64	3
Wiggins, Alan, Balt.†	.285	76	298	43	85	0	21	30
Wilfong, Rob, Cal.*	.189	83	217	16	41	4	13	4
Wilkerson, Curtis, Tex.†	.244	129	360	35	88	0	22	14
Willard, Jerry, Clev.*	.270	104	300	39	81	7	36	0
Wilson, Willie, K.C.†	.278	141	605	87	168	4	43	43
Winfield, Dave, N.Y.	.275	155	633	105	174	26	114	19
Wright, George, Tex.†	.190	109	363	21	69	2	18	4
Wynegar, Butch, N.Y.†	.223	102	309	27	69	5	32	0
Young, Mike, Balt.†	.273	139	450	72	123	28	81	1
Yount, Robin, Milw.	.277	122	466	76	129	15	68	10

AMERICAN LEAGUE
Pitching

(70 or more innings pitched)
*Throws Lefthanded

Pitcher and Club	W	L	ERA	G	IP	H	BB	SO
Aase, Don, Balt.	10	6	3.78	54	88.0	83	35	67
Acker, Jim, Tor.	7	2	3.23	61	86.1	86	43	42
Alexander, Doyle, Tor.	17	10	3.45	36	260.2	268	67	142
Atherton, Keith, Oak.	4	7	4.30	56	104.2	89	42	77
Bannister, Floyd, Chi.*	10	14	4.87	34	210.2	211	100	198
Beckwith, Joe, K.C.	1	5	4.07	49	95.0	99	32	80
Berenguer, Juan, Det.	5	6	5.59	31	95.0	96	48	82
Birtsas, Tim, Oak.*	10	6	4.01	29	141.1	124	91	94
Black, Bud, K.C.*	10	15	4.33	33	205.2	216	59	122
Blyleven, B., Clev.-Minn.	17	16	3.16	37	293.2	264	75	206
Boddicker, Mike, Balt.	12	17	4.07	32	203.1	227	89	135
Bordi, Rich, N.Y.	6	8	3.21	51	98.0	95	29	64
Boyd, Dennis, Bos.	15	13	3.70	35	272.1	273	67	154
Burns, Britt, Chi.*	18	11	3.96	36	227.0	206	79	172
Burris, Ray, Milw.	9	13	4.81	29	170.1	182	53	81
Butcher, John, Minn.	11	14	4.98	34	207.2	239	43	92
Clancy, Jim, Tor.	9	6	3.78	23	128.2	117	37	66
Clemens, Roger, Bos.	7	5	3.29	15	98.1	83	37	74
Cliburn, Stu, Cal.	9	3	2.09	44	99.0	87	26	48
Cocanower, Jamie, Milw.	6	8	4.33	24	116.1	122	73	44
Codiroli, Chris, Oak.	14	14	4.46	37	226.0	228	78	111
Cowley, Joe, N.Y.	12	6	3.95	30	159.2	132	85	97
Crawford, Steve, Bos.	6	5	3.76	44	91.0	103	28	58
Darwin, Danny, Milw.	8	18	3.80	39	217.2	212	65	125
Davis, Storm, Balt.	10	8	4.53	31	175.0	172	70	93
Dixon, Ken, Balt.	8	4	3.67	34	162.0	144	64	108
Easterly, Jamie, Clev.*	4	1	3.92	50	98.2	96	53	58
Filson, Pete, Minn.*	4	5	3.67	40	95.2	93	30	42
Fisher, Brian, N.Y.	4	4	2.38	55	98.1	77	29	85
Flanagan, Mike, Balt.*	4	5	5.13	15	86.0	101	28	42
Gibson, Bob, Milw.	6	7	3.90	41	92.1	86	49	53

Pitcher and Club	W	L	ERA	G	IP	H	BB	SO
Gubicza, Mark, K.C.	14	10	4.06	29	177.1	160	77	99
Guidry, Ron, N.Y.*	22	6	3.27	34	259.0	243	42	143
Haas, Moose, Milw.	8	8	3.84	27	161.2	165	25	78
Harris, Greg, Tex.	5	4	2.47	58	113.0	74	43	111
Heaton, Neal, Clev.*	9	17	4.90	36	207.2	244	80	82
Hernandez, Willie, Det.*	8	10	2.70	74	106.2	82	14	76
Higuera, Ted, Milw.*	15	8	3.90	32	212.1	186	63	127
Hooton, Burt, Tex.	5	8	5.23	29	124.0	149	40	62
Hough, Charlie, Tex.	14	16	3.31	34	250.1	198	83	141
Howell, Jay, Oak.	9	8	2.85	63	98.0	98	31	68
Hurst, Bruce, Bos.*	11	13	4.51	35	229.1	243	70	189
Jackson, Danny, K.C.*	14	12	3.42	32	208.0	209	76	114
James, Bob, Chi.	8	7	2.13	69	110.0	90	23	88
John, T., Cal.-Oak.*	4	10	5.53	23	86.1	117	28	25
Key, Jimmy, Tor.	14	6	3.00	35	212.2	188	50	85
Kison, Bruce, Bos.	5	3	4.11	22	92.0	98	32	56
Krueger, Bill, Oak.*	9	10	4.52	32	151.1	165	69	56
Lamp, Dennis, Tor.	11	0	3.32	53	105.2	96	27	68
Langston, Mark, Sea.*	7	14	5.47	24	126.2	122	91	72
Leibrandt, Charlie, K.C.*	17	9	2.69	33	237.2	223	68	108
Lollar, Tim, Chi.-Bos.*	8	10	4.62	34	150.0	140	98	105
Lopez, Aurelio, Det.	3	7	4.80	51	86.1	82	41	53
Martinez, Dennis, Balt.	13	11	5.15	33	180.0	203	63	68
McCaskill, Kirk, Cal.	12	12	4.70	30	189.2	189	64	102
McCatty, Steve, Oak.	4	4	5.57	30	85.2	95	41	36
McClure, Bob, Milw.*	4	1	4.31	38	85.2	91	30	57
McGregor, Scott, Balt.*	14	14	4.81	35	204.0	226	65	86
Moore, Donnie, Cal.	8	8	1.92	65	103.0	91	21	72
Moore, Mike, Sea.	17	10	3.46	35	247.0	230	70	155
Morris, Jack, Det.	16	11	3.33	35	257.0	212	110	191
Nelson, Gene, Chi.	10	10	4.26	46	145.2	144	67	101
Niekro, Phil, N.Y.	16	12	4.09	33	220.0	203	120	149
Nipper, Al, Bos.	9	12	4.06	25	162.0	157	82	85
Noles, Dickie, Tex.	4	8	5.06	28	110.1	129	33	59
Nunez, Edwin, Sea.	7	3	3.09	70	90.1	79	34	58
O'Neal, Randy, Det.	5	5	3.24	28	94.1	82	36	52
Ojeda, Bob, Bos.*	9	11	4.00	39	157.2	166	48	102

Pitcher and Club	W	L	ERA	G	IP	H	BB	SO
Petry, Dan, Det.	15	13	3.36	34	238.2	190	81	109
Quisenberry, Dan, K.C.	8	9	2.37	84	129.0	142	16	54
Rasmussen, D., N.Y.*	3	5	3.98	22	101.2	97	42	63
Righetti, Dave, N.Y.*	12	7	2.78	74	107.0	96	45	92
Romanick, Ron, Cal.	14	9	4.11	31	195.0	210	62	64
Rozema, Dave, Tex.	3	7	4.19	34	88.0	100	22	42
Ruhle, Vern, Clev.	2	10	4.32	42	125.0	139	30	54
Saberhagen, Bret, K.C.	20	6	2.87	32	235.1	211	38	158
Schmidt, Dave, Tex.	7	6	3.15	51	85.2	81	22	46
Schrom, Ken, Minn.	9	12	4.99	29	160.2	164	59	74
Schulze, Don, Clev.	4	10	6.01	19	94.1	128	19	37
Seaver, Tom, Chi.	16	11	3.17	35	238.2	223	69	134
Shirley, Bob, N.Y.*	5	5	2.64	48	109.0	103	26	55
Slaton, Jim, Cal.	6	10	4.37	29	148.1	162	63	60
Smithson, Mike, Minn.	15	14	4.34	37	257.0	264	78	127
Snell, Nate, Balt.	3	2	2.69	43	100.1	100	30	41
Spillner, Dan, Chi.	4	3	3.44	52	91.2	83	33	41
Stanley, Bob, Bos.	6	6	2.87	48	87.2	76	30	46
Stewart, Sammy, Balt.	5	7	3.61	56	129.2	117	66	77
Stieb, Dave, Tor.	14	13	2.48	36	265.0	206	96	167
Sutton, Don, Oak.-Cal.	15	10	3.86	34	226.0	221	59	107
Swift, Bill, Sea.	6	10	4.77	23	120.2	131	48	55
Tanana, F., Tex.-Det.*	12	14	4.27	33	215.0	220	57	159
Terrell, Walt, Det.	15	10	3.85	34	229.0	221	95	130
Thomas, Roy, Sea.	7	0	3.36	40	93.2	66	48	70
Viola, Frank, Minn.*	18	14	4.09	36	250.2	262	68	135
Vuckovich, Pete, Milw.	6	10	5.51	22	112.2	134	48	55
Waddell, Tom, Clev.	8	6	4.87	49	112.2	104	39	53
Wardle, C., Minn.-Clev.*	8	9	6.18	50	115.0	127	62	84
Whitson, Ed, N.Y.	10	8	4.88	30	158.2	201	43	89
Wills, Frank, Sea.	5	11	6.00	24	123.0	122	68	67
Witt, Mike, Cal.	15	9	3.56	35	250.0	228	98	180
Young, Matt, Sea.*	12	19	4.91	37	218.1	242	76	136

NATIONAL LEAGUE
Batting

(40 or more at-bats)
*Bats Lefthanded †Switch-Hitter

Batter and Club	AVG	G	AB	R	H	HR	RBI	SB
Adams, Ricky, S.F.	.190	54	121	12	23	2	10	1
Aguayo, Luis, Phil.	.279	91	165	27	46	6	21	1
Almon, William, Pitt.	.270	88	244	33	66	6	29	10
Anderson, David, L.A.	.199	77	221	24	44	4	18	5
Andujar, Joaquin, St.L.†	.106	38	94	2	10	0	8	3
Ashby, Alan, Hou.†	.280	65	189	20	53	8	25	0
Backman, Walter, N.Y.†	.273	145	520	77	142	1	38	30
Bailey, J. Mark, Hou. †	.265	114	332	47	88	10	45	0
Bailor, Robert, L.A.	.246	74	118	8	29	0	7	1
Bass, Kevin, Hou.†	.269	150	539	72	145	16	68	19
Bedrosian, Stephen, Atl.	.078	37	64	3	5	0	1	0
Bell, David, Cin.	.219	67	247	28	54	6	36	0
Benedict, Bruce, Atl.	.202	70	208	12	42	0	20	0
Bevacqua, Kurt, S.D.	.239	71	138	17	33	3	25	0
Bilardello, Dann, Cin.	.167	42	102	6	17	1	9	0
Bochy, Bruce, S.D.	.268	48	112	16	30	6	13	0
Bosley, Thaddis, Chi.*	.328	108	180	25	59	7	27	5
Bowa, L., Chi.-N.Y.†	.234	86	214	15	50	0	15	5
Braun, Stephen, St.L.*	.239	64	67	7	16	1	6	0
Bream, Sidney, L.A.-Pitt.*	.230	50	148	18	34	6	21	0
Brenly, Robert, S.F.	.220	133	440	41	97	19	56	1
Brock, Gregory, L.A.*	.251	129	438	64	110	21	66	4
Brooks, Hubert, Mtl.	.269	156	605	67	163	13	100	6
Brown, J. Christopher, S.F.	.271	131	432	50	117	16	61	2
Brown, Michael, C., Pitt.	.332	57	205	29	68	5	33	2
Brown, Rogers, S.D.†	.155	79	84	8	13	0	6	6
Browning, Thomas, Cin.*	.193	39	88	4	17	0	2	0
Bumbry, Alonza, S.D.*	.200	68	95	6	19	1	10	2
Butera, Salvatore, Mtl.	.200	67	120	11	24	3	12	0
Cabell, Enos, Hou.-L.A.	.272	117	335	40	91	2	36	9
Carter, Gary, N.Y.	.281	149	555	83	156	32	100	1

Batter and Club	AVG	G	AB	R	H	HR	RBI	SB
Cedeno, Cesar, Cin.-St.L.	.291	111	296	38	86	9	49	14
Cerone, Richard, Atl.	.216	96	282	15	61	3	25	0
Cey, Ronald, Chi.	.232	145	500	64	116	22	63	1
Chambliss, Chris., Atl.*	.235	101	170	16	40	3	21	0
Chapman, Kelvin, N.Y.	.174	62	144	16	25	0	7	5
Christensen, John, N.Y.	.186	51	113	10	21	3	13	1
Clark, Jack, St.L.	.281	126	442	71	124	22	87	1
Coleman, Vincent, St.L.†	.267	151	636	107	170	1	40	110
Concepcion, David, Cin.	.252	155	560	59	141	7	48	16
Corcoran, Timothy, Phil.*	.214	103	182	11	39	0	22	0
Cox, Danny, St.L.	.152	35	79	3	12	0	6	0
Cruz, Jose, Hou.*	.300	141	544	69	163	9	79	16
Darling, Ronald, N.Y.	.171	42	76	9	13	0	0	1
Daulton, Darren, Phil.*	.204	36	103	14	21	4	11	3
Davis, Charles, S.F.†	.270	136	481	53	130	13	56	15
Davis, Eric, Cin.	.246	56	122	26	30	8	18	16
Davis, Gerald, S.D.	.293	44	58	10	17	0	2	0
Davis, Glenn, Hou.	.271	100	350	51	95	20	64	0
Davis, Jody, Chi.	.232	142	482	47	112	17	58	1
Dawson, Andre, Mtl.	.255	139	529	65	135	23	91	13
Deer, Robert, S.F.	.185	78	162	22	30	8	20	0
DeJesus, Ivan, St.L.	.222	59	72	11	16	0	7	2
Denny, John, Phil.	.123	33	81	2	10	0	4	2
Dernier, Robert, Chi.	.254	121	469	63	119	1	21	31
Diaz, Baudilio, Phil.-Cin.	.245	77	237	21	58	5	31	0
Dilone, Miguel, Mtl.-S.D.†	.200	78	130	18	26	0	7	17
Doran, William, Hou.†	.287	148	578	84	166	14	59	23
Dravecky, David, S.D.	.116	34	69	5	8	0	1	0
Driessen, D., Mtl.-S.F.*	.243	145	493	53	120	9	47	2
Duncan, Mariano, L.A.†	.244	142	562	74	137	6	39	38
Dunston, Shawon, Chi.	.260	74	250	40	65	4	18	11
Durham, Leon, Chi.*	.282	153	542	58	153	21	75	7
Dykstra, Leonard, N.Y.*	.254	83	236	40	60	1	19	15
Eckersley, Dennis, Chi.	.125	26	56	1	7	1	1	0
Esasky, Nicholas, Cin.	.262	125	413	61	108	21	66	3
Fernandez, C. Sid., N.Y.*	.212	26	52	2	11	0	1	0
Fitzgerald, Michael, Mtl.	.207	108	295	25	61	5	34	5

Batter and Club	AVG	G	AB	R	H	HR	RBI	SB
Flannery, Timothy, S.D.*	.281	126	384	50	108	1	40	2
Foley, Thomas, Cin.-Phil.*	.240	89	250	24	60	3	23	2
Fontenot, S. Ray, Chi.*	.049	38	41	2	2	0	0	0
Forsch, Robert, St.L.	.244	34	45	3	11	1	4	0
Foster, George, N.Y.	.263	129	452	57	119	21	77	0
Francona, Terry, Mtl.*	.267	107	281	19	75	2	31	5
Frobel, Doug., Pitt.-Mtl.*	.189	65	132	17	25	1	11	4
Gainey, Telmanch, Hou.*	.162	13	37	5	6	0	0	0
Galarraga, Andres, Mtl.	.187	24	75	9	14	2	4	1
Garner, Philip, Hou.	.268	135	463	65	124	6	51	4
Garvey, Steven, S.D.	.281	162	654	80	184	17	81	0
Gladden, C. Daniel, S.F.	.243	142	502	64	122	7	41	32
Gonzalez, Denio, Pitt.	.226	35	124	11	28	4	12	2
Gooden, Dwight, N.Y.	.226	35	93	11	21	1	9	0
Gott, James, S.F.	.196	26	51	6	10	3	3	0
Green, David, S.F.	.248	106	294	36	73	5	20	6
Gross, Gregory, Phil.*	.260	93	169	21	44	0	14	1
Gross, Kevin, Phil.	.138	39	65	1	9	1	6	0
Guerrero, Pedro, L.A.	.320	137	487	99	156	33	87	12
Gullickson, William, Mtl.	.188	29	64	2	12	0	6	0
Gwynn, Anthony, S.D.*	.317	154	622	90	197	6	46	14
Hall, Albert, Atl.†	.149	54	47	5	7	0	3	1
Hammaker, C. At., S.F.†	.085	29	47	0	4	0	0	0
Harper, Brian, St.L.	.250	43	52	5	13	0	8	0
Harper, Terry, Atl.	.264	138	492	58	130	17	72	9
Hatcher, William, Chi.	.245	53	163	24	40	2	10	2
Hawkins, M. Andrew, S.D.	.078	33	77	1	6	0	3	0
Hayes, Von, Phil.*	.263	152	570	76	150	13	70	21
Hebner, Richard, Chi.*	.217	83	120	10	26	3	22	0
Heep, Daniel, N.Y.*	.280	95	271	26	76	7	42	2
Hendrick, George, Pitt.	.230	69	256	23	59	2	25	1
Hernandez, Keith, N.Y.*	.309	158	593	87	183	10	91	3
Herr, Thomas, St.L.†	.302	159	596	97	180	8	110	31
Hershiser, Orel, L.A.	.197	37	76	5	15	0	4	1
Hesketh, Joseph, Mtl.*	.091	26	44	0	4	0	1	0
Horner, J. Robert, Atl.	.267	130	483	61	129	27	89	1
Hoyt, D. LaMarr, S.D.	.063	31	64	4	4	0	2	0

Batter and Club	AVG	G	AB	R	H	HR	RBI	SB
Hubbard, Glenn, Atl.	.232	142	439	51	102	5	39	4
Hudson, Charles, Phil.†	.140	38	57	2	8	0	3	0
Hurdle, Clinton, N.Y.*	.195	43	82	7	16	3	7	0
Jeltz, L. Steven, Phil.	.189	89	196	17	37	0	12	1
Johnson, Howard, N.Y.†	.242	126	389	38	94	11	46	6
Jorgensen, Michael, St.L.*	.196	72	112	14	22	0	11	2
Kemp, Steven, Pitt.*	.250	92	236	19	59	2	21	1
Kennedy, Terrence, S.D.*	.261	143	532	54	139	10	74	0
Kepshire, Kurt, St.L.*	.118	32	51	6	6	0	2	0
Khalifa, Sam, Pitt.	.238	95	320	30	76	2	31	5
Knepper, Robert, Hou.*	.141	38	78	5	11	1	5	0
Knicely, Alan, Cin.-Phil.	.242	55	165	17	40	5	26	0
Knight, C. Ray, N.Y.	.218	90	271	22	59	6	36	1
Komminsk, Brad, Atl.	.227	106	300	52	68	4	21	10
Krenchicki, Wayne, Cin.*	.272	90	173	16	47	4	25	0
Krukow, Michael, S.F.	.218	28	55	2	12	1	3	1
LaPoint, David, S.F.*	.167	31	60	4	10	0	6	0
Lake, Steven, Chi.	.151	58	119	5	18	1	11	1
Landreaux, Ken., L.A.*	.268	147	482	70	129	12	50	15
Landrum, Terry, St.L.	.280	85	161	21	45	4	21	1
Law, Vance, Mtl.	.266	147	519	75	138	10	52	6
Lawless, Thomas, St.L.	.207	47	58	8	12	0	8	2
LeMaster, John, S.F.-Pitt.	.122	34	74	5	9	1	6	1
Leonard, Jeffrey, S.F.	.241	133	507	49	122	17	62	11
Lezcano, Sixto, Pitt.	.207	72	116	16	24	3	9	0
Lopes, David, Chi.	.284	99	275	52	78	11	44	47
Lynch, Edward, N.Y.	.077	31	52	1	4	0	0	0
Maddox, Garry, Phil.	.239	105	218	22	52	4	23	4
Madlock, Bill, Pitt.-L.A.	.275	144	513	69	141	12	56	10
Mahler, Richard, Atl.	.156	39	90	9	14	0	8	0
Maldonado, Candido, L.A.	.225	121	213	20	48	5	19	1
Marshall, Michael, L.A.	.293	135	518	72	152	28	95	3
Martinez, Carmelo, S.D.	.253	150	514	64	130	21	72	0
Matthews, Gary, Chi.	.235	97	298	45	70	13	40	2
Matuszek, Leonard, L.A.*	.222	43	63	10	14	3	13	0
Mazzilli, Lee, Pitt.†	.282	92	117	20	33	1	9	4
McGee, Willie, St.L.†	.353	152	612	114	216	10	82	56

Batter and Club	AVG	G	AB	R	H	HR	RBI	SB
McReynolds, W.K., S.D.	.234	152	564	61	132	15	75	4
McWilliams, Larry, Pitt.*	.125	32	40	2	5	0	2	0
Milner, Eddie, Cin.*	.254	145	453	82	115	3	33	35
Moreland, B. Keith, Chi.	.307	161	587	74	180	14	106	12
Morrison, James, Pitt.	.254	92	244	17	62	4	22	3
Mumphrey, Jerry, Hou.†	.277	130	444	52	123	8	61	6
Murphy, Dale, Atl.	.300	162	616	118	185	37	111	10
Nettles, Graig, S.D.*	.261	137	440	66	115	15	61	0
Nicosia, Steven, Mtl.	.169	42	71	4	12	0	1	1
Niekro, Joseph, Hou.	.250	32	68	6	17	0	6	0
Nieto, Thomas, St.L.	.225	95	253	15	57	0	34	0
Nokes, Matthew, S.F.*	.208	19	53	3	11	2	5	0
Oberkfell, Kenneth, Atl.*	.272	134	412	30	112	3	35	1
Oester, Ronald, Cin.†	.295	152	526	59	155	1	34	5
Oliver, Albert, L.A.*	.253	35	79	1	20	0	8	1
Orsulak, Joseph, Pitt.*	.300	121	397	54	119	0	21	24
Ortiz, Adalberto, Pitt.	.292	23	72	4	21	1	5	1
Owen, Lawrence, Atl.	.239	26	71	7	17	2	12	0
Paciorek, Thomas, N.Y.	.284	46	116	14	33	1	11	1
Pankovits, James, Hou.	.244	75	172	24	42	4	14	1
Parker, David, Cin.*	.312	160	635	88	198	34	125	5
Pena, Antonio, Pitt.	.249	147	546	53	136	10	59	12
Pendleton, Terry, St.L.†	.240	149	559	56	134	5	69	17
Perez, Atanasio, Cin.	.328	72	183	25	60	6	33	0
Perry, Gerald, Atl.*	.214	110	238	22	51	3	13	9
Porter, Darrell, St.L.*	.221	84	240	30	53	10	36	6
Puhl, Terrance, Hou.*	.284	57	194	34	55	2	23	6
Raines, Timothy, Mtl.†	.320	150	575	115	184	11	41	70
Rajsich, Gary, S.F.*	.165	51	91	5	15	0	10	0
Ramirez, Mario, S.D.	.283	37	60	6	17	2	5	0
Ramirez, Rafael, Atl.	.248	138	568	54	141	5	58	2
Rawley, Shane, Phil.	.138	36	58	3	8	0	6	0
Ray, Johnny, Pitt.†	.274	154	594	67	163	7	70	13
Redus, Gary, Cin.	.252	101	246	51	62	6	28	48
Reuschel, Ricky, Pitt.	.169	31	59	8	10	1	7	1
Reuss, Jerry, L.A.*	.135	34	74	1	10	0	7	0
Reynolds, G. Craig, Hou.*	.272	107	379	43	103	4	32	4

Batter and Club	AVG	G	AB	R	H	HR	RBI	SB
Reynolds, R., L.A.-Pitt.†	.282	104	337	44	95	3	42	18
Reynolds, Ronn, N.Y.	.209	28	43	4	9	0	1	0
Rhoden, Richard, Pitt.	.189	37	74	2	14	0	6	0
Roenicke, Ronald, S.F.†	.256	65	133	23	34	3	13	6
Rose, Peter, Cin.†	.264	119	405	60	107	2	46	8
Royster, Jeron, S.D.	.281	90	249	31	70	5	31	6
Runge, Paul, Atl.	.218	50	87	15	19	1	5	0
Russell, John, Phil.	.218	81	216	22	47	9	23	2
Russell, William, L.A.	.260	76	169	19	44	0	13	4
Ryan, L. Nolan, Hou.	.111	35	63	2	7	0	4	0
Samuel, Juan, Phil.	.264	161	663	101	175	19	74	53
Sandberg, Ryne, Chi.	.305	153	609	113	186	26	83	54
Santana, Rafael, N.Y.	.257	154	529	41	136	1	29	1
Sax, Stephen, L.A.	.279	136	488	62	136	1	42	27
Schmidt, Michael, Phil.	.277	158	549	89	152	33	93	1
Schu, Richard, Phil.	.252	112	416	54	105	7	24	8
Scioscia, Michael, L.A.*	.296	141	429	47	127	7	53	3
Scott, Michael, Hou.	.153	36	72	7	11	1	11	1
Shines, A.R., Mtl.†	.120	47	50	0	6	0	3	0
Show, Eric, S.D.	.127	35	79	3	10	1	6	0
Smith, Bryn, Mtl.	.194	32	72	6	14	1	4	0
Smith, Lonnie, St.L.	.260	28	96	15	25	0	7	12
Smith, Osborne, St.L.†	.276	158	537	70	148	6	54	31
Soto, Mario, Cin.	.133	37	83	3	11	0	4	0
Speier, Chris, Chi.	.243	106	218	16	53	4	24	1
Spilman, W. Harry, Hou.*	.136	44	66	3	9	1	4	0
Staub, Daniel, N.Y.*	.267	54	45	2	12	1	8	0
Stone, Jeffery, Phil.*	.265	88	264	36	70	3	11	15
Strawberry, Darryl, N.Y.*	.277	111	393	78	109	29	79	26
Sutcliffe, Richard, Chi.*	.233	20	43	4	10	1	3	0
Templeton, Garry, S.D.†	.282	148	546	63	154	6	55	16
Thomas, Derrel, Phil.†	.207	63	92	16	19	4	12	2
Thompson, Jason, Pitt.*	.241	123	402	42	97	12	61	0
Thompson, Milton, Atl.*	.302	73	182	17	55	0	6	9
Thompson, V., S.F.-Mtl.*	.224	98	143	10	32	0	10	0
Thon, Richard, Hou.	.251	84	251	26	63	6	29	8
Tibbs, Jay, Cin.	.092	36	65	3	6	0	3	0

Batter and Club	AVG	G	AB	R	H	HR	RBI	SB
Tolman, Timothy, Hou.	.140	31	43	4	6	2	8	0
Trevino, Alejandro, S.F.	.217	57	157	17	34	6	19	0
Trillo, J. Manuel, S.F.	.224	125	451	36	101	3	25	2
Trout, Steven, Chi.*	.109	24	46	2	5	0	2	0
Tudor, John, St.L.*	.138	37	94	9	13	0	2	0
Tunnell, B. Lee, Pitt.	.085	24	47	2	4	0	1	0
Uribe, Jose, S.F.†	.237	147	476	46	113	3	26	8
Valenzuela, F., L.A.*	.216	35	97	7	21	1	7	0
Van Gorder, David, Cin.	.238	73	151	12	36	2	24	0
Van Slyke, Andrew, St.L.*	.259	146	424	61	110	13	55	34
Venable, W. M., Cin.*	.289	77	135	21	39	0	10	11
Virgil, Osvaldo, Phil.	.246	131	426	47	105	19	55	0
Walker, Duane, Cin.*	.167	37	48	5	8	2	6	1
Wallach, Timothy, Mtl.	.260	155	569	70	148	22	81	9
Walling, Dennis, Hou.*	.270	119	345	44	93	7	45	5
Washington, C., Atl.*	.276	122	398	62	110	15	43	14
Washington, U.L., Mtl.†	.249	68	193	24	48	1	17	6
Webster, Mitchell, Mtl.†	.274	74	212	32	58	11	30	15
Welch, Robert, L.A.*	.180	25	50	4	9	0	4	0
Wellman, Brad, S.F.	.236	71	174	16	41	0	16	5
Whitfield, Terry, L.A.*	.260	79	104	8	27	3	16	0
Wilson, Glenn, Phil.	.275	161	608	73	167	14	102	7
Wilson, William, N.Y.†	.276	93	337	56	93	6	26	24
Winningham, H., Mtl.*	.237	125	312	30	74	3	21	20
Wohlford, James, Mtl.	.192	70	125	7	24	1	15	0
Woodard, Michael, S.F.*	.244	24	82	12	20	0	9	6
Woods, Gary, Chi.	.244	81	82	11	20	0	4	0
Wynne, Marvell, Pitt.*	.205	103	337	21	69	2	18	10
Yeager, Stephen, L.A.	.207	53	121	4	25	0	9	0
Youngblood, Joel, S.F.	.270	95	230	24	62	4	24	3
Zuvella, Paul, Atl.	.253	81	190	16	48	0	4	2

NATIONAL LEAGUE
Pitching

(40 or more innings pitched)
*Throws Lefthanded

Pitcher and Club	W	L	ERA	G	IP	H	BB	SO
Aguilera, Richard, N.Y.	10	7	3.24	21	122.1	118	37	74
Andersen, Larry, Phil.	3	3	4.32	57	73.0	78	26	50
Andujar, Joaquin, St.L.	21	12	3.40	38	269.2	265	82	112
Baller, Jay, Chi.	2	3	3.46	20	52.0	52	17	31
Barker, Leonard, Atl.	2	9	6.35	20	73.2	84	37	47
Bielecki, Michael, Pitt.	2	3	4.53	12	45.2	45	31	22
Blue, Vida, S.F.*	8	8	4.47	33	131.0	115	80	103
Botelho, Derek, Chi.	1	3	5.32	11	44.0	52	23	23
Browning, T., Cin.*	20	9	3.55	38	261.1	242	73	155
Brusstar, Warren, Chi.	4	3	6.05	51	74.1	87	36	34
Burke, Timothy, Mtl.	9	4	2.39	78	120.1	86	44	87
Calhoun, Jeffrey, Hou.*	2	5	2.54	44	63.2	56	24	47
Camp, Rick, Atl.	4	6	3.95	66	127.2	130	61	49
Campbell, William, St.L.	5	3	3.50	50	64.1	55	21	41
Candelaria, John, Pitt.*	2	4	3.64	37	54.1	57	14	47
Carlton, Steven, Phil.*	1	8	3.33	16	92.0	84	53	48
Carman, Donald, Phil.*	9	4	2.08	71	86.1	52	38	87
Castillo, Robert, L.A.	2	2	5.43	35	68.0	59	41	57
Cox, Danny, St.L.	18	9	2.88	35	241.0	226	64	131
Darling, Ronald, N.Y.	16	6	2.90	36	248.0	214	14	167
Davis, Mark, S.F.*	5	12	3.54	77	114.1	89	41	131
Dawley, William, Hou.	5	3	3.56	49	81.0	76	37	48
Dayley, Kenneth, St.L.*	4	4	2.76	57	65.1	65	18	62
Dedmon, Jeffrey, Atl.	6	3	4.08	60	86.0	84	49	41
DeLeon, Jose, Pitt.	2	19	4.70	31	162.2	138	89	149
Denny, John, Phil.	11	14	3.82	33	230.2	252	83	123
Diaz, Carlos, L.A.*	6	3	2.61	46	79.1	70	18	73
DiPino, Frank, Hou.*	3	7	4.03	54	76.0	69	43	49
Dravecky, David, S.D.*	13	11	2.93	34	214.2	200	57	105
Eckersley, Dennis, Chi.	11	7	3.08	25	169.1	145	19	117
Engel, Steven, Chi.*	1	5	5.57	11	51.2	61	26	29

Pitcher and Club	W	L	ERA	G	IP	H	BB	SO
Fernandez, C. Sid, N.Y.*	9	9	2.80	26	170.1	108	80	180
Fontenot, S. Ray, Chi.*	6	10	4.36	38	154.2	177	45	70
Forsch, Robert, St.L.	9	6	3.90	34	136.0	132	47	48
Forster, Terry, Atl.*	2	3	2.28	46	59.1	49	28	37
Franco, John, Cin.*	12	3	2.18	67	99.0	83	40	61
Frazier, George, Chi.	7	8	6.39	51	76.0	88	52	46
Garber, H. Eugene, Atl.	6	6	3.61	59	97.1	98	25	66
Garrelts, Scott, S.F.	9	6	2.30	74	105.2	76	58	106
Gooden, Dwight, N.Y.	24	4	1.53	35	276.2	198	69	268
Gorman, Thomas, N.Y.*	4	4	5.13	34	52.2	56	18	32
Gossage, Richard, S.D.	5	3	1.82	50	79.0	64	17	52
Gott, James, S.F.	7	10	3.88	26	148.1	144	51	78
Gross, Kevin, Phil.	15	13	3.41	38	205.2	194	81	151
Guante, Cecilio, Pitt.	4	6	2.72	63	109.0	84	40	92
Gullickson, W., Mtl.	14	12	3.52	29	181.1	187	47	68
Hammaker, C. At., S.F.*	5	12	3.74	29	170.2	161	47	100
Hawkins, M.A., S.D.	18	8	3.15	33	228.2	229	65	69
Heathcock, R. J., Hou.	3	1	3.36	14	56.1	50	13	25
Hershiser, Orel, L.A.	19	3	2.03	36	239.2	179	68	157
Hesketh, Joseph, Mtl.*	10	5	2.49	25	155.1	125	45	113
Holland, A., Phil.-Pitt.*	1	4	3.45	41	62.2	53	21	48
Honeycutt, F., L.A.*	8	12	3.42	31	142.0	141	49	67
Horton, Ricky, St.L.*	3	2	2.91	49	89.2	84	34	59
Howell, Kenneth, L.A.	4	7	3.77	56	86.0	66	35	85
Hoyt, D. LaMarr, S.D.	16	8	3.47	31	210.1	210	20	83
Hudson, Charles, Phil.	8	13	3.78	38	193.0	188	74	122
Hume, Thomas, Cin.	3	5	3.26	56	80.0	65	35	50
Jackson, Roy Lee, S.D.	2	3	2.70	22	40.0	32	13	28
Johnson, Joseph, Atl.	4	4	4.10	15	85.2	95	24	34
Kepshire, Kurt, St.L.	10	9	4.75	32	153.1	155	71	67
Kerfeld, Charles, Hou.	4	2	4.06	11	44.1	44	25	30
Knepper, Robert, Hou.*	15	13	3.55	37	241.0	253	54	131
Koosman, J., Phil.*	6	4	4.62	19	99.1	107	34	60
Krukow, Michael, S.F.	8	11	3.38	28	194.2	176	49	150
Lahti, Jeffrey, St.L	5	2	1.84	52	68.1	63	26	41
LaPoint, David, S.F.*	7	17	3.57	31	206.2	215	74	122
Laskey, W., S.F.-Mtl.	5	16	4.91	30	148.1	165	53	60

Pitcher and Club	W	L	ERA	G	IP	H	BB	SO
Leach, Terry, N.Y.	3	4	2.91	22	55.2	48	14	30
Lefferts, Craig, S.D.*	7	6	3.35	60	83.1	75	30	48
Lucas, Gary, Mtl.*	6	2	3.19	49	67.2	63	24	31
Lynch, Edward, N.Y.	10	8	3.44	31	191.0	188	27	65
Mahler, Michael, Mtl.*	1	4	3.54	9	48.1	40	24	32
Mahler, Richard, Atl.	17	15	3.48	39	266.2	272	79	107
Mathis, Ronald, Hou.	3	5	6.04	23	70.0	83	27	34
McDowell, Roger, N.Y.	6	5	2.83	62	127.1	108	37	70
McGaffigan, A., Cin.	3	3	3.72	15	94.1	88	30	83
McMurtry, J. Craig, Atl.	0	3	6.60	17	45.0	56	27	28
McWilliams, Larry, Pitt.*	7	9	4.70	30	126.1	139	62	52
Meridith, Ronald, Chi.*	3	2	4.47	32	46.1	53	24	23
Minton, Gregory, S.F.	5	4	3.54	68	96.2	98	54	37
Niedenfuer, Thomas, L.A.	7	9	2.71	64	106.1	86	24	102
Niekro, Joseph, Hou.	9	12	3.72	32	213.0	197	99	117
Orosco, Jesse, N.Y.*	8	6	2.73	54	79.0	66	34	68
Palmer, David, Mtl.	7	10	3.71	24	135.2	128	67	106
Pastore, Frank, Cin.	2	1	3.83	17	54.0	60	16	29
Perez, Pascual, Atl.	1	13	6.14	22	95.1	115	57	57
Power, Ted, Cin.	8	6	2.70	64	80.0	65	45	42
Price, Joseph, Cin.*	2	2	3.90	26	64.2	59	23	52
Rawley, Shane, Phil.*	13	8	3.31	36	198.2	188	81	106
Reardon, Jeffrey, Mtl.	2	8	3.18	63	87.2	68	26	67
Reuschel, Ricky, Pitt.	14	8	2.27	31	194.0	153	52	138
Reuss, Jerry, L.A.*	14	10	2.92	34	212.2	210	58	84
Rhoden, Richard, Pitt.	10	15	4.47	35	213.1	254	69	128
Roberge, Bertrand, Mtl.	3	3	3.44	42	68.0	58	22	34
Robinson, Don, Pitt.	5	11	3.87	44	95.1	95	42	65
Robinson, Ronald, Cin.	7	7	3.99	33	108.1	107	32	76
Rucker, David, Phil.*	3	2	4.31	39	79.1	83	40	41
Ruthven, Richard, Chi.	4	7	4.53	20	87.1	103	37	26
Ryan, L. Nolan, Hou.	10	12	3.80	35	232.0	205	95	209
St. Claire, Randy, Mtl.	5	3	3.93	42	68.2	69	26	25
Sanderson, Scott, Chi.	5	6	3.12	19	121.0	100	27	80
Schatzeder, Daniel, Mtl.*	3	5	3.80	24	104.1	101	31	64
Scott, Michael, Hou.	18	8	3.29	36	221.2	194	80	137
Scurry, Rodney, Pitt.*	0	1	3.21	30	47.2	42	28	43

Pitcher and Club	W	L	ERA	G	IP	H	BB	SO
Shields, Stephen, Atl.	1	2	5.16	23	68.0	86	32	29
Show, Eric, S.D.	12	11	3.09	35	233.0	212	87	141
Sisk, Douglas, N.Y.	4	5	5.30	42	73.0	86	40	26
Smith, Bryn, Mtl.	18	5	2.91	32	222.1	193	41	127
Smith, David, Hou.	9	5	2.27	64	79.1	69	17	40
Smith, Lee, Chi.	7	4	3.04	65	97.2	87	32	112
Smith, Zane, Atl.*	9	10	3.80	42	147.0	135	80	85
Sorensen, Lary, Chi.	3	7	4.26	45	82.1	86	24	34
Soto, Mario, Cin.	12	15	3.58	36	256.2	196	104	214
Stoddard, Timothy, S.D.	1	6	4.65	44	60.0	63	37	42
Stuper, John, Cin.	8	5	4.55	33	99.0	116	37	38
Sutcliffe, Richard, Chi.	8	8	3.18	20	130.0	119	44	102
Sutter, H. Bruce, Atl.	7	7	4.48	58	88.1	91	29	52
Tekulve, K., Pitt.-Phil.	4	10	3.57	61	75.2	74	30	40
Thurmond, Mark, S.D.*	7	11	3.97	36	138.1	154	44	57
Tibbs, Jay, Cin.	10	16	3.92	35	218.0	216	83	98
Trout, Steven, Chi.*	9	7	3.39	24	140.2	142	63	44
Tudor, John, St.L.*	21	8	1.93	36	275.0	209	49	169
Tunnell, B. Lee, Pitt.	4	10	4.01	24	132.1	126	57	74
Valenzuela, F., L.A.*	17	10	2.45	35	272.1	211	101	208
Walk, Robert, Pitt.	2	3	3.68	9	58.2	60	18	40
Welch, Robert, L.A.	14	4	2.31	23	167.1	141	35	96
Williams, Frank, S.F.	2	4	4.19	49	73.0	65	35	54
Winn, James, Pitt.	3	6	5.23	30	75.2	77	31	22
Wojna, Edward, S.D.	2	4	5.79	15	42.0	53	19	18
Youmans, Floyd, Mtl.	4	3	2.45	14	77.0	57	49	54

BRUCE WEBER PICKS
HOW THEY'LL FINISH IN 1986

American League East

1. New York
2. Toronto
3. Baltimore
4. Detroit
5. Boston
6. Cleveland
7. Milwaukee

American League West

1. California
2. Chicago
3. Kansas City
4. Minnesota
5. Seattle
6. Oakland
7. Texas

National League East

1. New York
2. Montreal
3. St. Louis
4. Philadelphia
5. Chicago
6. Pittsburgh

National League West

1. Los Angeles
2. San Diego
3. Cincinnati
4. Houston
5. Atlanta
6. San Francisco

American League Champions: New York Yankees
National League Champions: New York Mets
World Champions: New York Yankees

YOU PICK
HOW THEY'LL FINISH IN 1986

American League East

1.
2.
3.
4.
5.
6.
7.

American League West

1.
2.
3.
4.
5.
6.
7.

National League East

1.
2.
3.
4.
5.
6.

National League West

1.
2.
3.
4.
5.
6.

American League Champions:

National League Champions:

World Champions: